SYMBOLISM

ON

GREEK COINS

by

Agnes Baldwin

Sanford J. Durst
Numismatic Publications
New York, N.Y.

FOREWORD

Agnes Baldwin (Brett) needs no further introduction to lovers of Greek art and Greek coinage. She was born in the centennial of American independence, and she died at her home near Boston eighty years later, having just seen her epic *Catalogue of Greek Coins* in the Museum of Fine Arts, Boston, through the press. Hers was a life singularly devoted to Greek and Roman numismatics in their purest form, chiefly at the American Numismatic Society in New York during the decades made great by the life, collecting, and writings of her slightly-younger contemporary Edward T. Newell.

In her unusual monograph *Symbolism on Greek Coins*, Agnes Baldwin attempted to reconcile numismatics, archaeology, art, primitivism, and psychology in a way which must have seemed advanced in 1916 (at least in America if not in Central Europe). These studies fell out of fashion in the more circumscribed numismatic and archaeological disciplines of 1920 to 1960 and later, and they have only come back into full, serious fashion in the past decade. The subject of symbolism involves a wide spectrum of ideas derived from the shorthand images, designs, and special letters on Greek archaic or classical coins, and the multitude of retrospective compositions, motifs, and symbols embraced by the quasi-autonomous Greek cities of Asia Minor, Syria, and Egypt under the Roman Empire. Mrs. Brett also belonged to the age of Sir Arthur Evans (he who was no mean numismatist and collector of rare Greek and Roman coins) and Mrs. Harriet Boyd Hawes. Their discoveries among the Minoan and Mycenaean palaces and towns of Crete showed her astute numismatic eye the timeless past of the incuse heraldry on early Greek coins. Add the Egyptian survivals on the coins of the eastern end of the Mediterranean and the crypto-Christianity (or Jewish symbolism) buried in numerous Greek imperial inscriptions, reverse-types and cult-symbols, and Greek coins became to Mrs. Brett a complex index of religious, moral, and physical aspirations evident in many other arts of Greece, Rome, and Byzantium.

In substance, Mrs. Brett applied numismatics to the realms of abstract thought, and the results have become a classic of modern scholarship fully worthy of appreciation in the last decades of the second millennium of the Christian era. She dared to speculate, to imagine, to synthesize in ways timid specialists would avoid, and *Symbolism on Greek Coins* is once again available to the serious numismatist as a document of numismatic humanism in the long tradition from Winckelmann through Imhoof-Blumer and Gardner to the scholars of *architectura numismatica* in our own time.

CORNELIUS C. VERMEULE III
Curator of Classical Art
Museum of Fine Arts, Boston,
and Harvard University

SYMBOLISM ON GREEK COINS

Introduction. Symbol and Myth

THE FISH SYMBOL IN CHRISTIAN ART

The explanation of the symbols employed by peoples of past ages in their art, in which usually religious conceptions are expressed, has often proved a difficult matter. The fish symbolism in Christian art, for instance, is a typical example of one of the oddities of religious expression whose interpretation has been found baffling.[1] The intention of the symbolism is perfectly plain, the fish represents Christ. But the origin of this parallelism is obscure. The traditional explanation of the rise of the symbol from the well-known ΙΧΘΥΣ-acrostic ΙΗΣΟΥΣ ΧΡΙΣΤΟΣ ΘΕΟΥ ΥΙΟΣ ΣΩΤΗΡ, Ἰησοῦς Χριστὸς Θεοῦ Υἱὸς Σωτήρ, 'Jesus Christ, Son of God, Saviour,' has not been considered satisfactory. For, one instinctively realizes that the acrostic, an expansion of the Greek word for fish, must be subsequent to the symbolism. The formal adoption both of acrostic and pictorial symbol as mystic emblems might have been coincidental, but it cannot be supposed that the whole symbolic conception arose solely out of the acrostic.

R. Mowat[2] derived the symbol from the acrostic formula which he thought was invented by the Christians of Alexandria at the time of the persecutions under Domitian (81-96 A. D.), as an answer to the deification of the Roman Emperor appearing on the Imperial coins

---

[1] R. Forrer, Reallexicon der prähistorischen, classischen und frühchristlichen Altertümer, 1907, art. Fische, says, "Der Ursprung dieser Inparallelestellung ist noch unklar." C. R. Morey, The Origin of the Fish Symbol, Princeton Theological Review, 1910–1912, "Of all the symbols by which the early Christians attempted to embody, and at the same time perhaps to conceal, the concepts of their faith, the Fish is the most obscure in point of origin." (Introd.)

[2] R. Mowat, Bull. de la Soc. nat. des antiquaires de France, 1898 (Summary on pp. 121, 122); Atti del II Congresso inter. di Roma, 1902, pp. 1–8.

struck in this city, ΑΥΤ ΚΑΙϹ ΘΕΟΥ ΥΙΟϹ ΔΟΜΙΤ ϹΕΒ ΓΕΡΜ. The phrase ΘΕΟΥ ΥΙΟϹ (= DIVI F[ilius] on Roman Imperial coins) means 'Son of the Deified (Emperor)', not 'Son of God' as in the acrostic. However, one should not beg the question of Imperial deification which was tacitly acknowledged during the life-time of the reigning emperor as well as openly concurred in after his death. It was only one step more from the cult of the dead to that of the living emperor.[1] The Christians of Alexandria may therefore have seen in the phrase an implication of divinity.

But Alexandria was not the original home of the symbolism, the monuments on which it first occurs being found in Rome.[2] Again, it is doubtful if the symbolism was known as early as the First Century A. D. There are no monuments bearing it which can be dated much before the middle of the Second Century. Furthermore, the fish symbol is not mentioned in the Physiologus (ὁ Φυσιολόγος), a work on animal symbolism written by an Alexandrian Greek about the first half of this same Century. This treatise is a sort of Natural History, a compendium of marvellous tales explaining the mystical meanings of animals and plants with moral applications, a kind of theological zoology and botany. If the fish symbol was in use at the time of this allegorical manual, we should certainly expect to find it here recorded. The Christian fathers, too, before Tertullian, end of the Second Century, make no reference to the symbol. It is safe to assume, then, that the symbolism was not widely current in Rome until about 150 A. D. (round date). Mowat's theory which is full of improbabilities, and extremely artificial, would not require more than passing notice if it were not for the fact that it has been adopted as the generally accepted interpretation in a recent handbook on Christian archaeology of considerable authority, (K. M. Kaufmann, Handbuch der christlichen Archäologie, 1913).

Even if we supposed that prior to the acrostic, Christ was usually called Ἰησοῦς Χριστὸς Θεοῦ Υἱὸς Σωτήρ, and that the abbreviation Ι·Χ·Θ·Υ·Σ being commonly seen on the monuments (a pure hypothesis), the Ichthys-symbolism and the acrostic were thus accidentally suggested, there would still remain the necessity of explaining what mental predisposition could render a symbol, thus artificially devised, acceptable. It is far more reasonable to assume that the acrostic was an ingenious afterthought invented either to explain what was mysterious to the

---

[1] Mrs. Eugénie Sellers Strong, Apotheosis and After-Life, London, 1915.

[2] See below, note 4, page 92.

early Christians themselves or to clothe the symbol in more hieratic garb. As Morey puts it, the acrostic was adopted ' to crystallize an association of ideas into more dogmatic expression.' The 'Ιχθύς-acrostic stands to the symbol as a rationalizing of the emblem, perhaps imperfectly understood by the Christians at large. But it could not explain the riddle to them, if riddle it was, nor does it now to us.

The 'Ιχθύς-formula is first known to us from the Sibyllina Oracula, a late work composed of elements of various dates. The acrostic occurs in the eighth book of the Oracula in verses 217-250, the initial letters of the words which start lines 217-243, read downwards, giving the formula of five words; the following seven lines, 244-250 (probably a later addition) forming the word ΣΤΑΥΡΟΣ ' Cross.' This part of Book VIII of the Oracula (vv. 217-250) belongs to an earlier stratum than the rest of the compilation, being assigned to the latter half of the Second Century. The symbolism, at all events, is definitely proved to have been in use before the end of the Second Century, by the reference in Tertullian, De Baptismo, ch. 1 (c. 200 A. D.), in which the author employs the expression ' 'Ιχθύν nostrum, Iesum Christum.' This direct allusion without explanation shows that his readers were already acquainted with the Ichthys-symbolism as designating Christ, and seems to imply, though it does not definitely prove, the pre-existence of the acrostic. The Aberkios inscription dated c. 160-180 A. D., and the Licinia Amias epitaph, Fig. A, c. 155 A. D., as we shall see, prove that the Ichthys-symbolism was known c. 150 A. D. and they also afford strong presumption that the acrostic was then in use. The acrostic was doubtless invented shortly after the pictorial symbol came into use.

If the symbolism did not have its origin in the acrostic[1] how is it to be interpreted? Investigators have examined the Old and New Testaments for light on the symbol,[2] and have also sought to derive it from a pagan prototype. But no meaning thus far proposed has won general recognition, and the symbol has remained an enigma. To recall the Babylonian semi-fish bodied deity Ea (or Oannes), or the Phoenician

---

[1] This is the view of most investigators. H. Usener, Sintflutsagen, p. 224, " hielt es für allein denkbar dass, weil das Bild des Fisches lebendig und verbreitet war, klügelnder Witz sich das griechische Wort beschaute und ihm durch jene anagrammatische Entdeckung nur tiefere Bedeutung verlieh " (cited by F. J. Dölger, 'Ιχθύς; das Fischsymbol in frühchristlichen Zeit, Bd. I, 1910, p. 52). So also, S. Reinach, Orpheus, 1909, p. 20, note 1.

[2] " Old and New Testaments have been ransacked for prototypes, the writings of the fathers have been carefully reviewed, antiquity has been searched for parallels, and every department of early Christian history, thought and custom has been laid under contribution, but the question seems still as far from solution as ever." (Morey, *op. cit.* Introd., p. 93.)

Dagon, or the fish cults of Syria is of no avail, because the analogy is imperfect,[1] and furthermore the contact cannot be established. According to the archaeological evidence, the rings, seals, gold-glasses, catacomb inscriptions, etc., on which the symbol and the Ἰχθύς-abbreviation occur, Rome was the place of origin. R. Pischel[2] went so far afield in his search as Tibet where he tried to show contact between certain Christian communities and Brahman and Buddhist sects in whose myths the fish symbolized the rescuer or saviour, and also became the ritual food. None of these outside derivations, from Semites, or Syrian Greeks, or Indians has any convincing arguments to substantiate a theory of tradition, nor is it at all likely that the early Christians would have consciously adopted a symbol from pagan cults[3] by a deliberate process of borrowing. By this last statement we do not deny the continued existence of pagan mythical concepts and symbols during the early Christian era, a fact only too well attested by the monuments. The old religious symbolism was too deeply rooted to disappear entirely. But it was, in some sort, assimilated to the new religion, and a mere indication of cultic practices in pagan antiquity vaguely resembling the fish symbolism, without proof of syncretic absorption, is per se an improbable derivation. It is not surprising, in view of the difficulties which beset the problem of the fish symbolism that the most judicious writers have not countenanced a pagan origin, but have sought for the explanation in Christian thought and practice. Nevertheless, as will later be argued, a pagan source through the medium of a pagan-Christian legend, is the most convincing solution.[4]

[1] In the ancient fish worship, eating of the sacred fish was restricted to a particular caste, the priests, whereas the fish in Christian religion was the prescribed ritual food for all believers.

[2] Der Ursprung des christlichen Fischsymbols, Sitzungsberichte der königl. Preuss. Akad. d. Wissenschaften, 1905, pp. 506 ff.

[3] I. Scheftelowitz, Das Fisch-Symbol im Judentum und Christentum, Archiv für Religionswissenschaft, 14 Bd., 1911, traces the symbol to a Jewish prototype.

[4] The fact that the symbolism was expressed by the Greek word Ἰχθύς offers strong presumption that it arose among a Greek-speaking population. Now it appears to have had its greatest prevalence among the Christians at Rome, a Latin-speaking people. It must therefore have been brought to them from Greek-speaking peoples, else why should not the word *piscis* have been adopted by the uneducated classes with whom Christianity took its first hold? The earliest literary sources available containing clear and definite allusion to the Ichthys-symbolism hail from the East, the Aberkios epitaph, a Greek inscription on a stone from Phrygia, and the Ἐξήγησις τῶν πραχθέντων ἐν Περσίδι, a dialogue in dramatic form with the scene laid at the court of the Sassanidae. These documents, as our argument developes, taken in connection with the Greek name for the symbol, justify our tracing the ultimate home of the symbol to the Greeks of the Eastern part of the Roman world, and not to those of Alexandria, as Mowat did, for which latter place evidence is completely lacking.

Morey's authoritative contribution to the problem, a comprehensive and critical review of all the evidence, contains the final conclusion that the testimony of the earliest Christian writers who mention the symbol, and the direct allusion in the Aberkios inscription favor the view that the fish symbolism was originally of eucharistic significance. Morey points to the importance attached by the early church to the Multiplication, or miracle of the loaves and fishes, and to the Supper at the Sea of Tiberias. It is necessary then to explain how the double bread-and-fishes symbol came to be replaced by the Fish alone. For, while part of the literary and monumental evidence tends to establish the eucharistic symbolism of the fish, still this meaning is not the only one. It is therefore not quite clear just how Christ came to be later equated absolutely with the Ichthys. Morey's account of this evolution, which presents his exact position on the question of the relation of the acrostic formula to the symbolism, is as follows. He believes that the symbolism was derived ultimately from the Multiplication, and that prior to the acrostic it meant only the eucharist. This meaning is seen in the frescoes of the Lucina catacomb on which fish and baskets full of bread loaves (and in the centre of each basket, a chalice of wine) are painted.[1] As the symbolism progressed, he thinks, artistic reasons gave greater prominence to the fish over the bread. But, he adds, " it is at least questionable if such an association of ideas could ever have evolved, independently of the acrostic, the later definite concept of the Fish=Christ " . . . . " There is every reason to suppose therefore that the fish as a definite symbol of Christ owes its origin to the acrostic." Out of the general eucharistic symbolism there developed the more special Christ=Fish symbol due to the introduction of the Ichthys-acrostic. This position involves a theory of the independent origin of the acrostic distinct from the fish as an emblem of the eucharist, and in addition an effort is made to show from the monuments the secondary and later character of the simpler symbolic equation, Christ=Fish.

The monuments anterior to the introduction of the acrostic, should witness only to the eucharistic meaning. This hypothesis would seem to be at once contradicted by the well-known Licinia Amias epitaph on which are depicted two fishes with anchor between, with the Greek inscription ΙΧΘΥC ΖΩΝΤΩΝ ' Fish of the Living, i. e. the Believers,' Fig. A. Here there is no trace of the eucharistic fish-symbolism. The monument

---

[1] Morey, op. cit, 1912, pl. I, 1. The painting belongs to the early Second Century.

Fig. A.

is dated by Dölger, c. 155 A. D.,[1] or before the generally accepted date
of the acrostic formula, c. 200 A. D. Opinions differ as to the early date
claimed for the monument by Dölger and others, but assuming that it
should be assigned to the middle of the Second Century, how would
this accord with the theory? Well, Morey rejects this monument as
being no true example of the absolute equation Christ=Fish, for the
reason that there are two fishes represented, and they cannot possibly
stand for the symbol. However, it does not seem at all improbable
that considerations of symmetry led to the two-fish arrangement. The
two-fish-anchor type alone would not, as Morey insists, be a certain
instance of the Christian symbolism, but with the legend IXΘYC ZⲰNTⲰN,
the symbolic meaning is certain. The whole idea of the hope of immortality, *spes in Christo*, the faith of the believers in Christ, is evident
in picture and Greek inscription.

Morey would disconnect pictorial symbol from inscription, discount
the former because two fishes can not stand for Christ, and explain the
latter in the following way. The first word is regarded as equivalent
to I·X·Θ·Υ·C, that is, as not being the word Ἰχθύς at all, but simply
the customary abbreviation of the name and titles of Christ, which he
assumes to have existed and at a date previous to that of this inscription, and to be quite independent of the symbolism and the later acrostic formula. But this interpretation is exceedingly strained, and far
too dubious to be seriously considered. The epitaph can not be put

---

[1] *Op. cit.* p. 161 (published in Religionsgeschichtliche u. epigraphische Untersuchungen,
Supplement to Römische Quartalschrift für christliche Alterthumskunde), 1910.

aside as not representing the Christ=Fish symbolism. If then its early date be admitted (and Morey does not contest it), the monument constitutes a grave objection to his hypothesis that the Christ=Fish symbol was evolved out of a supposed earlier eucharistic symbolism[1] solely under the influence of the subsequently invented Ichthys-acrostic.

The interpretation which will here be advocated is just the reverse of the above as regards order of development, the absolute symbol Christ=Fish seeming to us to precede the later eucharistic meaning. But it does not necessitate any division of the monuments into two chronological groups according to the different forms of the symbolism, for, given the equation Christ=Fish, the eucharistic significance could enter immediately into the concept. Once the Fish had become the mystic symbol of Christ and of everlasting life, its ritual use as food symbolizing union of the believer with God would spring almost simultaneously into being. Both elements of the symbolism were bound up in the secondary or eucharistic sense, but there is no ground from the data at our disposal for arguing that this latter sense was the earlier. The fundamental meaning was the primary one, and that survived the longest. It is found in the Pektorios inscription which has been dated anywhere from the Second to the Sixth Century,[2] and, conspicuously, in the employment of the Ichthys-symbol as a prophylakterion over the entrances to houses and graves down to a rather late period.[3]

The basic difficulty, Christ=Fish, which has never really been surmounted, disappears completely with the new interpretation. Furthermore, the document containing the earliest allusion to the symbol known to us in Christian literature, the epitaph of Aberkios (c. 160-180 A. D.) is our chief support in the line of contemporary testimony. Not only the Aberkios inscription, but also the language of one closely contemporary writer, Tertullian, is found upon examination in the light of the new meaning, to allude to a different significance which will clarify the symbolic, mystical equation. Also, the late anonymous work, Narratio rerum quae in Perside acciderunt, confirms the sense which seems to us to be the original one.[4]

---

[1] The painting of the Lucina catacomb which is cited in support of this contention, and dated before 150 A. D., i. e. before the Licinia Amias stele, is not really an example of the fish symbolism under discussion, but merely a representation of the Multiplication.

[2] O. Pohl, Das Ichthys-Monument von Autun, 1880.

[3] Dölger, *op. cit.* p. 273.

[4] This is the same work under its Latin title, as the ἘΞήγησις referred to above in note 4, p. 92. It is of late date, but based upon much earlier sources (cf. Morey, *op. cit.*).

Now this particular symbol has been chosen as an introduction to the discussion of the nature of symbols, for the reason that it has generally been regarded hitherto as enigmatical. Its meaning has remained veiled to us because up to the present its psychological content has not been grasped. This is true of a great number of symbols. Only recently psychological investigation has revealed those hidden processes of the human mind which have conditioned the expression of religious emotion in the form of symbolism. A solution by means of the new psychological theory will afford strong justification of the scientific value and soundness of the new hypothesis.

PSYCHOLOGICAL INTERPRETATION OF MYTHS AND SYMBOLS

Before proceeding to state what the ultimate significance of the fish symbol is, a brief account of this new theory must be given. We might say that it is not so much a theory as a way of looking at things. This way of looking at symbols is new because it has been determined by a new insight into the human soul, and it is therefore a psychological theory of the origin of symbols. Within the past fifteen years, a group of psychologists in Germany have been investigating the phenomena of nervous and mental diseases, paranoia, hysteria, dementia praecox and other psychoneuroses which are pathological psychic manifestations, the analysis of which has brought with it a profound knowledge of the inner psychic life of man. A new method called the psychoanalytic was thereby developed, and led to the observation of normal psychic phenomena in an entirely new light.

Sigmund Freud was the leader of this new school. In his Drei Abhandlungen zur Sexualtheorie 1905,[1] his treatises, Der Witz und seine Beziehung zum Unbewussten, 1905, and, Der Wahn und die Träume in W. Jensen's ' Gradiva ' 1907, various apparently unrelated expressions of the human psyche are shown to have a common origin in the unconscious life of the soul, in the life of childhood and in sexuality.[2] A particularly illuminating contribution to that slightly explored region of mental life was his work, Die Traumdeutung, 1900, (4th edit. 1914).[3] The elaboration of the ' wish theory ' of dreams and

---

[1] Translated by A. A. Brill, Nervous and Mental Disease Monograph Series, No. 7, New York, 1910.

[2] For summaries in English, see I. H. Coriat, Abnormal Psychology, New York, 1914, and K. Abraham, Dreams and Myths, New York, 1913, Ner. and Men. Dis. Mon. Ser., No. 15= Traum und Mythus, Schriften zur angewandten Seelenkunde, Leipzig and Vienna, 1909.

[3] The English translation is by A. A. Brill, The Interpretation of Dreams, 3rd edit., New York, 1913.

its bearing on the psychology of myths puts us in a position to understand the products of the human mind, in religion, art, poetic fancy
and symbolic conceptions, as never before. A most brilliant application of Freud's teachings, together with a wonderfully original, syn-
thetic study of the products of the human genius in art and religion, is
C. G. Jung's Wandlungen und Symbole der Libido, Leipzig and Vienna,
1912.[1] Freud's and Jung's contributions to psychological theory are
no whit less revolutionary and profoundly important than the Darwin-
ian hypothesis. What the theory of evolution means in the physical
world, psychoanalysis means in the psychic.

It must not lightly be objected by archaeologists that the psychological interpretation is 'purely subjective,' and therefore not admis-
sible. When we say 'subjective,' nothing *arbitrarily* subjective is
intended. By this we mean, that tendency of some mystics who
read a double meaning into everything, quite irrespective of any general law of the human mind. Such interpretations of symbols have
long fallen into discredit among scholars.[2] Modern psychology and
philosophy teach us that the usual antithesis between 'objective' and
'subjective' is more apparent than real. A good expression of this
idea is the following: "It is not that we have two contrasted worlds,
the 'objective' and the 'subjective'; there is but one world, the objective, and that which we have hitherto not understood, have dubbed
therefore the 'subjective', are the subtler workings of integrated objective mechanisms," (E. B. Holt, The Freudian Wish and its Place
in Ethics, p. 93, 1915). That is to say, psychic phenomena as well as
physical, belong to the category of things determined by natural law.
The phenomena of symbolism are the reaction of the human psyche to
the external world, and the meaning of such reaction as expressed in
symbolism can be known, if we can discover the laws of mental life.
This fact had long ago been recognized by the great psychologist Wundt,
in regard to myths which are created by the same associative or ana-

---

[1] English translation, Psychology of the Unconscious, by Dr. Beatrice M. Hinkle, New York, 1916 (Moffat, Yard & Co.).

[2] For a case of the highly subjective viewpoint evolved entirely out of one's own person-ality, see Adólph Roeder's Symbol Psychology, New York, 1913, an example of subjective inter-pretation which is just the antithesis of Thomas Inman's Ancient Pagán and Modern Christian Symbolism, and due solely to the personal bias of the author. A parallel case of the same type of interpretation is one from the Thirteenth Century, Guilielmus Durandus (1220–1296), Rationale divinorum officiorum, trs. by Neale and Webb, The Symbolism of Churches and Church Orna-ments, New York, 1893. In this work, every portion of the church is said to have symbolic significance; the cement is love and charity binding together the stones which represent the faithful, etc.

logical processes as symbols. "Die letzte Quelle aller Mythenbildung, aller religiösen Gefühle und Vorstellungen ist die individuelle Phantasietätigkeit," he remarks in his discussion on Die Phantasie als allgemeine seelische Funktion, ch. 1 of Völkerpsychologie, 1905, 2 Bd., pt. 1, p. 3ff.

Myths and symbols are very closely related, they are both symbolic presentations or substitutes, resembling that for which they stand. The myth is an imaginary tale, a word-picture; and the symbol is an ideograph, either in the form of a simple diagrammatic image (thunderbolt of Zeus, the weather-deity), or in the shape of a natural object (eagle of Zeus, the sky-god; and also, in some cults, an analogue of the sun-god). The problem is consequently to determine what is back of the disguised formation. And, for both myth and symbol presentations, since they have arisen in prehistoric times, one must get back to the subjective phantasies of primitive man.

It may be thought that the fish symbolism in Christian art can have nothing to do with the psyche of primitive man. If, namely, it can be proved that the symbol as the Christians used it has no relation to antiquity,[1] there is no need of invoking primitive phantasy. Modern science answers with the biological law that the individual in his separate life repeats the life-history of the race. This is true, we now know, of man's psychical evolution as well as of his physical. Moreover, the general intellectual level of the early Christians as a whole must have been uncommonly like that of early man in the matter of religious or emotional reactions towards life. This attitude of mind resulting in unconscious symbolism is well expressed by Émile Male.[2] Speaking of the later Middle Ages he says, "The Thirteenth Century believed that all the world was one vast symbol, a sort of divine cipher. The stars, the seasons, shadow and light, the course of the sun reflected upon a wall, the rhythm of numbers, plant and animal life, all was resolved into a concept. One might say of this marvelous world with Shakespeare, that it was 'made of the same stuff as our dreams.'"

[1] Thus Morey derives the symbolism from actual events in Christian times from the eucharist, out of the Multiplication. But he feels this derivation inadequate to account for the definite equation Christ=Fish, and hence assumes the acrostic as the real determining factor, which practically takes us back to the traditional explanation. The deeper intent of the symbolism has therefore not been found in Christian history or custom. Symbols are of course of two distinct kinds; the more obvious, rational sort which constitutes a kind of tachygraphy or short-hand representation of a larger, more complicated concept or subject, and the less obvious, mystical kind which has its roots in the emotions. This latter symbolism springs largely from the unconscious and is less intelligible at first view. The Christ=Fish symbolism is clearly of the latter variety.

[2] Revue de l'Art Ancien et Moderne, 1908, L'Art Symbolique à la fin du Moyen Age.

The mediaeval Bestiaries or Beast-books which passed for scientific literature in those days, afford a striking indication of the subjective habit of thought of the period, in addition to the fantastic symbolism in art.[1] The people of the Middle Ages believed in the actual existence of fabulous animals, the unicorn, the phoenix and other impossible creatures, and accepted as ancient history the mythical romances woven about the heroic figures of Alexander the Great and the legendary Aeneas. Perhaps not since the dawn of history has there been an epoch in which the people at large, had this relation to the objective world. It was in the Eleventh, Twelfth and Thirteenth Centuries particularly that excessive animal symbolism was employed in church architecture. The protest of St. Bernard (c. 1125), registered in an open letter to the Church, contained the following query: "What mean those filthy apes, those fierce lions, those monstrous centaurs, those half-men, those spotted tigers, those fighting soldiers and horn-blowing monsters?" The efforts of this refined ecclesiastic were unavailing, however, to stem the tide of coarse allegory which reached its zenith, and then losing its vitality as a popular menagerie (doubtless always with some admixture of humorous appeal) was adapted to the purposes of vulgar satire directed against the Jews and the reformers of the Sixteenth Century.

Modern writers on this subject explain this phenomenon of animal symbolism in Christian art as a survival. This is true, for it is indeed a survival, but from within, not from without as commonly understood. Mrs. A. Kemp-Welch,[2] for example, suggests that it was "the outcome of Oriental tradition through unconscious copying or irrepressible semi-conscious paganism,"[3] or else "the result of the treatises on symbolic animals." But the latter explanation, though intended to suggest another cause, is tantamount to the survival theory. For, one cannot explain the phenomenon of symbolic literature of this sort which was written and seriously accepted as descriptive of objective realities, in any other way than that of symbolism in art. Such a work as the Physiologus (cf. p. 90) which belongs to the Second Century and was the model for all the later Christian allegories, the Bestiaria, Lapidaria and Volucraria which constituted the popular science of the Middle Ages, would never have attained its position as an authoritative book

[1] E. P. Evans, Animal Symbolism in Ecclesiastical Architecture, New York, 1896.

[2] Beast Imagery and the Bestiary, Nineteenth Century, 1903.

[3] This part of the explanation offers a choice between objective and subjective survival.

on Natural History,[1] if the people had not been largely given to subjective thinking. Just as the artist looks upon the external world as a symbol, so the people of the mediaeval period were in general under the spell of an imaginative conception of a world born solely of their emotions. This phenomenon will be analyzed subsequently. For the moment we are only concerned to maintain, what the history of art and of culture abundantly and obviously prove, namely, that symbolism is a psychological characteristic of the whole human race. Phylogenetically regarded, it is a 'survival' of our primitive soul-life. Undoubtedly the Bestiaries and their ilk reacted powerfully to stimulate the innate craving for symbolic expression, and created new forms besides those inherited from antiquity. The symbolic literature was itself, however, created to satisfy the same inner necessity as the art types.

So the fish symbol, even though as a matter of fact it can be shown to have had an historical precedent, as a psychological possibility, might have arisen in our own era as well as in antiquity. If we find that the Christian art of the earliest centuries manifests to lesser degree the animal symbolism which ran riot at the climax of mediaeval culture, two reasons may be advanced to account for this difference. In the first place, a conscious protest and scruple against the continuation of pagan symbols would naturally lead to their temporary and almost complete exclusion. But the fundamental reason would be that a substitute had been found for religious emotional needs. The great symbol of the Christ-figure at first overshadowed all traditional symbols. Then, as the irrepressible impulse to symbolize sought further outlet, the figures of the Virgin and the Saints arose to satisfy the need for increased expression.[2]

[1] The Physiologus was translated into Latin, Aethiopic, Syriac, Armenian, Icelandic, Anglo-Saxon, and all the principal European languages and dialects, and with the exception of the Bible, was the most widely read book of any time. The Christian apologists accepted its teachings as scientific truth, and reinforced their dogmas from its moral allegory. Despite its preposterous zoology, it had a tremendous vogue among the educated who never questioned its manifest absurdity. In the Fourth Century, to be sure, it was condemned by some of the more enlightened Church fathers, but was reinstated by Gregory the Great.

[2] If we turn to the Byzantine coinage on which, as a result of the conversion of Constantine the Great to the new faith, Christian emblems first appear, we observe that the Cross and the Christ-monogram are the earliest symbols of the new religion (c. 314 A. D.). These symbols and the figure of Christ as a coin-type (c. 700 A. D.) preceded the introduction of the Virgin (c. 892 A. D.) and the Saints (Tenth and Eleventh Centuries). In the later mediaeval coinage of Italy, the figures of the Saints far outnumber the representations of Christ and the Virgin, (G. Macdonald, Coin Types, pp. 228 and 238). Since the selection of ancient coin-types was con-

Theriomorphic symbols, though less numerous at first than in pagan art, are not entirely absent. The dove, fish and lamb are early introduced. Pagan animal symbolism, though at first partially excluded, persisted nevertheless on a lower substratum, so to speak, in popular cults. The hoofed and horned devil is of course reminiscent of Pan. Symbolism was rife on all sides, as it must necessarily be in every religion, and it will occasion no surprise therefore when we discover that such ancient pagan symbols as the Swastika and the Ankh received a new lease of life through their adoption by the Christians.

In order to grasp more precisely the new psychological interpretation of symbols, which is the main subject of the present and succeeding articles, its bearing on the meaning of myths must first be briefly treated. Comparative mythology which was founded by Adalbert Kuhn[1] about fifty years ago, paved the way for a general interpretation of all myths. All myths, those of ancient civilized races and modern barbaric peoples, were shown to be substantially alike in general outline, and often amazingly similar in detail. The conclusion naturally followed that they must mean something common to all humanity. There has always been the greatest difficulty, however, in explaining the so-called 'irrational' elements in the myths of civilized peoples. The Greeks themselves, as we know, felt extremely apologetic in regard to many barbaric elements in their mythology, and felt constrained to say that it was all allegory. The battle of the gods and the giants, which the civilized Greek felt to be unseemly, was explained as a battle of the natural elements.

Passing over the earlier modern theories of Max Müller and Herbert Spencer which are no longer entertained,[2] we come to the view which regards myths as a figurative expression of religious ideas mingled with primitive attempts at an explanation of nature. Some writers feeling the futility of imputing ethical, abstract conceptions to primitive man, such as Preller-Robert's reduction of the Titan myth, with its monstrous detail of the unmanning of Uranos by Kronos, to the

trolled by a great conservatism, the coins having a public character and reflecting general religious thought, the order in which the Christian emblems were introduced is surely not without significance. It may therefore indicate the organic growth of Christian symbolism.

[1] Die Herabkunft des Feuers und des Göttertrankes, 1886. For a summary of Kuhn's contribution to mythology, see O. Gruppe, Culte und Mythen, cited below.

[2] Art. Mythology, Enc. Brit. Eleventh Edit., 1910, by Andrew Lang, (a repetition of the article in the edition of 1883.) The best general accounts of theories about the origin of myths and cults are to be found in O. Gruppe, Die Griechische Culte und Mythen in ihren Beziehungen zu den orientalischen Religionen, 1887, I, ch. 1, and W. Wundt, Völkerpsychologie, 1905, Bd 2, pt. 1, ch. 3.

generalized meaning 'that all higher order is the result of the strife of conflicting powers,' or Welcker's explanation which touches on the barbarous detail, that 'it meant creation removed from time, a symbol of the manifold diversity of created things,' have gone over to a specialized nature theory.[1] The myths are all astronomical allegories, some say, lunar, others, solar.[2] This theory contains much that is alluring, and has many adherents, as solar and lunar elements are undeniably present in many myths.

The position of mythologists in general on the astral theory is summed up by R. Wünsch,[3] as follows: "Dass aus Vorgängen am Himmel Mythen enstanden sind, wird kein Einsichtiger leugnen." Speaking of the real progress made by the science of mythology, in spite of apparent divergences of theory, he says (p. 602), "das Ausgehen von den Tatsachen der historischen Überlieferung, die vorsichtige Ausdeutung und *psychologische Erklärung*, unter Heranziehung verwandter Erscheinungen bei anderen Völkern, beginnt mehr Boden zu erobern Nun muss noch die Einseitigkeit überwunden werden die *alles nur astral* oder als *babylonisch* deutet", (the italics are the writer's).

One could not deprecate too strongly the one-sidedness of solar and lunar hypotheses, when the extraordinary pitch of absurdity is reached that dragon-contests, which had just been acceptably explained as solar (myth of the solar-hero), are claimed by the moon-myth adherents as illustrations of their view. E. Siecke, Drachenkämpfe, 1907, solemnly assures us that all mythical dragon-contests are moon myths; the moon is a serpent, and Asklepios is *therefore* a moon god![4]

The relation of the psychological interpretation to the astronomical is that the myth contains different component parts in which analysis may discern a stratification indicative of growth. The deepest

---

[1] For the psychological interpretation of the Titan myth, see E. F. Lorenz, Das Titanen-Motiv in der allgemeinen Mythologie, Imago, Zeitschrift für Anwendung der Psychoanalyse auf die Geisteswissenschaften, 1913, 1 Heft.

[2] H. Winckler, Himmels-und Weltenbild der Babylonier als Grundlage der Welt- Anschauung und Mythologie aller Völker, 1902.

[3] Griechische u. Römische Religion, 1906–1910, Archiv für Religionswissenschaft, 14 Bd., 1911. This is a report on the contributions to the science of mythology for the years 1906–1910; the previous summary being that of A. Dieterich for the years 1903–1905, *op. cit.* 8 Bd., 1905. The best general reference for the earlier bibliography is O. Gruppe, Die Mythologische Literatur aus den Jahren 1898–1905, Jahresbericht über die Fortschritte der klass. Alterthumswissenschaft, v. 137, Supplementband, 1908.

[4] So also the well-known symbols of the sun-disk between bull's horns in Egyptian representations of Isis, and even the Egyptian winged disk, always interpreted as sun-pictures, are explained as pictures of the *full moon!* E. Siecke, Götterattribute und Sogenannte Symbole, 1909, p. 199.

layer is that in which sexual symbolism is found. The upper layers have been created by various secondary factors, among which astronomical considerations play a leading part. It is the 'projection to the sky' of the phantasy, which has its root in sexual symbolism. Thus we may find the Whale Myth on the whole, solar, but this is not its deepest psychological intent. "Whale Myths, as psychoanalysis proves, are birth myths according to their latent content, but according to their manifest content, astral myths ", (E. F. Lorenz, Das Titanen-Motiv, p. 38).

Other mythologists, still avoiding the inexplicable, say that all the ' savage, silly and senseless details,' as Max Müller called them, are due to the fact that stories like these seemed natural to savages. The weakness of this explanation is that it does not tell us how it came about that ' primitive metaphysics ' could be tolerated in an age which had supposedly grown out of animism. Alexander the Great was many generations removed from prehistoric man, but even he, denying his earthly parent after the fashion of all heroes, explained his divine descent as from Zeus Ammon, and typified the divine birth by the union of his mother Olympias with a serpent. How could Alexander have made use of ' savage ' imagery, if he were not psychically predisposed towards the same sort of comparison? A similar tale was related of the births of Aristomenes, the legendary Spartan hero, and of the following historical characters, Aratos of Sikyon (b. 271 B. C.), Scipio Africanus Major (b. 234 B. C.) and Augustus, the first Roman Emperor.[1] The symbolism of generation by a serpent, then, is not confined to mythical prehistory, and modern psychoanalytic research has established that such symbolism is still present in the human psyche. Though no longer expressed in naive myths, and already repressed from consciousness among civilized peoples, the symbol crops up again from the depths of the repressed unconscious in the form of dreams, or, in neuroses, in actual imaginings. The conclusion becomes obvious that there is a fundamental identity of the human mind, independent of time and place, and that we are still united, in our psychological life, by insoluble bonds connecting us with antiquity.

---

[1] J. G. Frazer, Adonis, Attis and Osiris, The Golden Bough, IV[1], 1914, p. 81. It is significant that according to Suetonius, Atia, the mother of Augustus, dreamed of the future event, as did also Octavius, the father. (On oracular dreams see L. Deubner, De Incubatione, Giessen, 1899.) The content of each dream is given by Suetonius, Divus Augustus, 94: Eadem Atia prius quam pararet somniavit, intestina sua ferri ad sidera explicarique per omnem terrarum et caeli ambitum. Somniavit et pater Octavius, utero Atiae iubar solis exortum.

This leads naturally to a discussion of the two modes of thinking characteristic of the human consciousness, namely, directed or ordered thought which follows reality, and so-called phantasy thinking. A far-reaching analysis of the dream has revealed a completely unknown section of the human soul. Our dreams are phantasy thoughts similar to the phantasy activities of primitive man, of childhood, of poetic imagination, and of neuroses. In our conscious life there are always these two habits of thought, the phantasy activity and directed thinking. The latter, phylogenetically considered, is a later evolution of the human consciousness which antiquity, even in the full development of intellectual life as seen in Greek civilization at its highest, did not possess in the same measure as we moderns. The ancient Greeks who attained a high degree of culture, possessed the same innate intellectual capacity for directed thinking but, as they lived at an earlier cultural epoch, there was less demand for the exercise of this faculty. In brief, they did less directed thinking on the whole than we modern people are forced to do as a result of our social environment. Our modern science, as an intellectual technique, is the best example of the capacity for directed thinking, viewed both as a process, divested of the subjective and emotional, and as a psychological achievement.

Directed thinking, like concentration of any sort, is the result of effort and is fatiguing. Phantasy thinking, on the other hand, is easy and effortless. It is the characteristic way of thinking of the child, and of primitive man, also of the adult individual in the semi-conscious activity of dream-states, and of those disturbances of conscious activity, known as neuroses in their milder form, and as various forms of dementia in pronounced derangements. Subjective thinking which belongs to our phylogenetic past, is found in the unconscious life of all modern minds. From this kind of thinking, poetry, art, religion and philosophy have been created, and also the symbolism which is an inseparable accompaniment of these forms of emotional expression. Therefore only through an understanding of this subjective phantasy thinking, can the meaning of symbols, which are rooted in the unconscious, be revealed. Our day-dreams also lift us from reality on the same delightfully irresponsible, emotional flights. In dreams, repressed, egoistic fancies find expression which are in contrast to reality. The dream, according to the Freudian hypothesis, is the expression of a wish which has been excluded or repressed from consciousness. Upon this wish theory of dreams has been built the psychological meaning of the myth as a parallel development of the same wish-fulfilling tendency. The myth is the expression of the typical wishes of the mass-soul, just as the dream is that of the individual psyche. It is a survival from the childhood of the race, and because we have not heretofore understood infantile soul-life, the latent content of the myth has been hidden from us. Just as dreams in their manifest content, often seem absurd, so the myths of civilized peoples present seemingly irrational, and even monstrous, elements which have defied explanation.

What now are the revelations of psychoanalysis which will enable us to understand symbols and myths in a new way? A very brief answer may be given as follows: Man stands to lifeless objects in a subjective relation which springs from his sexuality.[1] Or again, " Sexual symbolism, I assert, is a psychological phenomenon of mankind at all times and in all places."[2] Or in a word, " Man sexualizes everything."[3] The example of the fish symbolism, as we shall see, will forestall any idea that by sexual we mean phallic. There are symbols, ancient and modern, which are grossly and unequivocally phallic, but the vast majority of symbolic presentations represent the sexual object in the form of a veiled analogue. In fact, that is the purpose of the act of symbolizing, to conceal the sexual interest in a non-sexual comparison. When we use the word ' purpose ' we do not imply a consciously determined, intellectual aim. Man is governed by an unconscious impulse to express his emotions in symbolisms or analogies which are unconsciously determined, and not intellectually derived, but spontaneously or involuntarily conceived. He does not so much deliberately try to conceal his emotional interest, as to express it in as many forms as possible.

JUNG'S THEORY OF THE LIBIDO SYMBOLISM

The general conception of symbols as Libido pictures, Libido comparisons, elaborated by Jung, will define the interpretation. By Libido, Jung means energy or force, but Freud's use of the term is in its original sense of sexual impulse. The latter has the concept of a bundle of impulses in which the Libido or the sexual impulse figures as a partial impulse of the whole system. Jung however widens the concept, and has developed it into a genetic concept of psychic energy, or an ' energic concept of psychological values.' It is analogous though not exactly similar to Bergson's ' élan vital.' The Libido concept thus approaches closely to the philosophical concept of Will. " In the multiplicity of natural phenomena we see the Will, the Libido, in its most

[1] Cf. Abraham, Dreams and Myths, p. 18.　　　　[2] Id. ib. p. 14.
[3] Kleinpaul, cited by Abraham, ib. p. 14.

varied application and form. We see the Libido in the stage of infancy at first wholly in the form of the nourishment impulse which is concerned with the rearing of the body. With the development of the body, there arise successively new fields of application of the Libido. The final field, dominating all other fields in its functional meaning, is sexuality which at first appears as extraordinarily bound up in the nourishment function.

In the field of sexuality the Libido attains that definition whose overwhelming importance justifies us entirely in the scientific use of the term, Libido.   Here the Libido is manifestly a procreation impulse; at first, essentially in the form of an undifferentiated sexual Urlibido which as life-force drives mankind directly to generation. (The clearest distinction of the two forms of Libido application is found in those animals among which the nourishment stage is separated from the sexual stage by a chrysalis stage.) From that sexual Urlibido which created the millions of eggs and seeds out of a tiny embryo, there have developed, with powerful restriction of fertility, certain derivatives whose function is maintained by a specially differentiated Libido. This differentiated Libido is now ' desexualized,' inasmuch as it is dissociated from its original function of the egg and sperma creation ; and, furthermore, there is no longer any possibility of bringing it back again to its original function. Thus the process of evolution in general consists in an increasing transformation of the Urlibido which generated merely continuity products, into the secondary functions of sex-attraction and protection of offspring." (Jung, *op. cit.*, pp.128, 129.)

From this rather abstract statement, we see that Jung conceives of the Libido as an Urlibido, or primary life-force, and as a manifestation of the will to live, to create. Thus when we speak of Libido pictures, we mean those images which are symbolic fulfillments of life-longings, of primitive Urlibido, or expression of the impulse to create. The hero, for example, is a Libido symbol, for he is a mythical concept, a projected embodiment of human desires, who in his typical fate reproduces the human Libido and its typical fate.[1] The Libido concept is so broad that the tree, the horse, the lion, the ram, the bull, a sun-picture may all be included, if they reflect the Libido symbolism, that is, if they are figurative expressions of vital force, as, for instance, of fertility or generation, death and immortality. The Libido symbol is not to be understood by its anatomical analogy, but by its *psychological*

---

[1] Otto Rank, Der Mythus von der Geburt des Helden, Schriften zur angew. Seelenkunde, 5 Heft, 1909.

analogy. For example, the Earth as Mother, the Heavens as Father, are Libido symbols.

Thus the Tree of Life and the Cross which in the earlier interpretations were always mysteriously identified as phallic emblems, need not be so considered necessarily. A Libido analogue may take on a specifically phallic meaning, that is, it may be applied in a narrower sexual sense. But, that purely phallic imagery is always to be seen in the various forms of the cross symbol,[1] the Egyptian Ankh, the Greek cross, Tau-cross, swastika, etc., is a theory entirely unsupported by external evidence from monumental sources, and without justification from *a priori* psychological reasoning. It was this literal meaning, current in the earlier literature of symbolism, that more reserved critics refused to accept, and rightly, for, as symbolism arises primarily from the unconscious, by so much the more vague are the analogies employed. Man clothes his sex symbols as a rule in non-sexual dress. Gross or literal sex images are themselves Libido symbols.[2]

What is true of symbols, applies equally to myths. The success of the psychological interpretation of myths may be judged in a given instance by its application to the Titan myth by E. F. Lorenz (*op. cit.,* cf. p. 102, note 1), and to the Prometheus myth by K. Abraham.[3] It was the Oedipus myth, however, in which this psychological method was first tested by Freud (Traumdeutung, pp. 185ff.). The success of this attempt to prove that the myth represents the fulfillment of repressed sexual wishes, was the starting-point for the analyses of a number of other myths, saga and fairy-tales, and the result has been the complete scientific justification of the workings of the psychological factors in myths. The new interpretation has to be brought into some relation with the former nature and religio-philosophical meanings. This is a complex question, as indeed the unravelling of any myth must be. Myths were never stationary, but were always forming and reforming with the changing social environment and ethical evolution. Each separate typical myth must be analyzed, just as the various symbols must be studied individually. Abraham's reconciliation of the nature mythological elements and the psychological meaning

---

[1] Sha Rocco, The masculine cross, and ancient sex worship; Thomas Inman, Ancient Pagan and Modern Christian Symbolism, 1874.

[2] Compare the Indian case cited in the preface to Goblet d'Alviella's book, The Migration of Symbols, 1896, p. xix.

[3] Dreams and Myths. Compare also the following, for an analysis of the Prometheus story, H. Steinthal, Die Ursprüngliche Form der Sage von Prometheus, Zeitschrift f. Völkerpsychologie und Sprachwissenschaft, Bd. 2, 1862, and A. Kuhn, Die Herabkunft des Feuers, etc.

is indicated in his account of the Prometheus myth. Briefly summed up, the nature mythological meaning of the myths is regarded as but part of the explanation. The impulse for self-preservation creates the nature meaning, the sexual impulse creates the fulfillment (in myth) of typical sex-wishes. For a more elaborate discussion see Lorenz (*op. cit.* pp. 70-72).[1]

Not only in the field of mythology, but also in the analysis of the lives of historical personages, the new method is applied with amazing results which make certain pages of history read like a romance. Freud's study of Leonardo da Vinci[2] gives us a possible clue to the interpretation of the mysterious Mona Lisa. And what shall we say of the analysis of the life and character of an Egyptian Pharoah who lived in the Fourteenth Century B. C. by the same methods as the dreams of normal man, or the phantastic imaginings of neurotic sufferers by a psychiatrist of to-day? One may judge for himself of the value of the psychoanalytic method by comparing the two accounts of this Pharoah, Amenhotep IV (1375-1358 B.C.), written recently by a savant and man of letters, on the one hand,[3] and by a psychoanalyst, on the other.[4] Both biographers employed the same historical material, chiefly the Tell-el-Amarna letters, newly discovered, which enabled them, with the help of hieroglyphic texts of the period, to reconstruct the life of the so-called heretic King. The more profound, more convincing explanation of the peculiarities of character of this eccentric ruler, who temporarily substituted monotheism for polytheism in Egyptian religion, is that of Abraham, and must, it seems, be accepted by an unprejudiced mind, as scientifically correct.

THE FISH — A LIBIDO SYMBOL

The long-deferred explanation of the fish symbol may now be given. The fish in the Christian analogy is the symbol of the 'child,' and for that reason the 'son' of God was called the Ichthys.[5] A parallel from antiquity is the fact that the son of Atargatis, or Astarte, the Syrian Mother Goddess, was named Ichthys.[6] The sense of the

---

[1] Cf. also O. Rank, Der Mythus von der Geburt des Helden.

[2] Eine Kindheitserinnerung des Leonardo da Vinci, Schriften zur angewandten Seelenkunde, 7 Heft, 1910.

[3] M. A. Moret, La revolution religieuse d'Aménophis IV, Annales du Musée Guimet, v. 31, 1909.

[4] K. Abraham, Amenhotep IV (Echnaton), Imago, 1912.

[5] Jung, Wandlungen u. Symbole d. Libido, pp. 190 ff., 210, 402.

[6] Roscher, Lexikon, s. v. Ichthys. Some scholars have derived the name of Tammuz, son of Ishtar, the Babylonian counterpart of Atargatis, from a phrase meaning " true Son of the deep water," Frazer, Adonis, p. 7.

20

symbolism, fish=child, is clearly seen in the Christian legend, which is preserved for us in the Aberkios inscription, a contemporary document. This inscription is the epitaph of a Christian of Hierapolis in Phrygia who lived in the Second Century. That part of the inscription[1] relating to the fish symbol runs as follows:

$$\text{Πίστις πάντη δὲ προῆγε} \qquad 12$$
$$\text{καὶ παρέθηκε τροφὴν πάντη ἰχθὺν ἀπὸ πηγῆς}$$
$$\text{πανμεγέθη καθαρόν, ὃν ἐδράξατο παρθένος ἁγνή}$$
$$\text{καὶ τοῦτον ἐπέδωκε φίλοις ἔσθειν (?) διὰ παντὸς} \qquad 15$$
$$\text{οἶνον χρηστὸν ἔχουσα κέρασμα διδοῦσα μετ' ἄρτου.}$$

" Faith was everywhere my guide and always offered me as food the fish from the fountain, the very great one, the pure one, which the Holy Virgin caught.   And this (i. e. the fish) she (Faith) gave to the friends (Believers) to eat everywhere, giving an excellent wine mixed with water — and bread as well."

The symbolic meanings of the fish, as the child, which the believers reverenced as the pure fish from the spring (or fountain) which the Holy Virgin caught, and of the fish, as the eucharist of which the believers partook, are both herein contained.   The Fish is most plainly the Virgin's son, for the catching of the fish by the Virgin, coupled with the expression, *the pure one*, is very obviously a veiled, i. e. symbolic, allusion to immaculate conception.   The inscription confirms then clearly enough the eucharistic significance of the Fish, but it shows also a symbolism which, as has been pointed out in the Astarte-Ichthys parallel, was a heritage from pagan times.   It is no wonder then that some critics have denied the inscription a Christian origin,[2] and have attempted the thesis that the Παρθένος ἁγνή was the Mother Goddess of antiquity, and the Ἰχθύς her son, Attis.   The attempt to impugn the Christian character of the epitaph did not succeed, however, for it is now accepted by the preponderance of authority as a Christian document of the highest importance.

How then have the critics understood the allusion to the Virgin catching the Fish from the fountain? Dölger and H. Achelis,[3] who are

---

[1] The epitaph is in autobiographical form, the author, Aberkios himself, relates how he went to Rome, and visited Syria; then comes the passage above-quoted, which is followed by the customary greetings, farewell, etc.

[2] G. Ficker, Der Heidnische Charakter der Abercius-Inschrift, Sitzsungsber. der k. preuss. Akad. der Wiss., 1894. A. Harnack, Zur Abercius-Inschrift, Texte und Untersuchungen zur Gesch. der altchr. Literatur, XII Bd., 1895. So also, H. Hepding, Attis, Seine Mythen und Sein Kult, Giessen, 1903, following A. Dieterich, Die Grabinschrift des Aberkios, Leipzig, 1896.

[3] Das Symbol des Fisches, 1888.

advocates of a baptismal significance as the ultimate source of the fish symbolism, see in the allusion a figurative way of saying that the Church (=Holy Virgin), seized (ἐδράξατο) the Fish, i. e. Christ, baptized in the Jordan. Morey discusses this theory only to reject it, but his disposal of the phrase 'from the fountain,' as offering "no more difficulty in interpretation than any other picturesque epithet (*sic*)" is hardly satisfactory. The whole phraseology itself, he thinks, shows the eucharistic sense. "The *one, very great*, pure fish which the holy Virgin caught, and with which the φίλοι are fed, can hardly be a real fish, and must be understood as a symbol."[1] This is satisfactory. That the Fish is Christ is also an inevitable conclusion. But is the Holy Virgin here the Church? Morey does not admit this. Seeing the difficulty of explaining the phrase ἀπὸ πηγῆς, Morey elsewhere says that "it may well be, as Duchesne says, a poetic phrase introduced to save the meter." It is precisely, as he says, these "two obscure points in the passage namely, the phrases ἀπὸ πηγῆς, 'from the fountain,' and ὃν ἐδράξατο παρθένος ἁγνή 'which the Holy Virgin seized,'" which are the stumbling blocks.

The symbolism of the Virgin catching the Fish is a Libido symbolism whose general type is revealed in the phenomena of unconscious symbolism familiar to psychoanalysis, and it would probably have remained forever a 'hidden' meaning if psychoanalysis had not come to our aid with its wonderful generalization of the Libido analogy. It all becomes clear when we have the key. On 'water' as a Libido analogy for the 'Mother,' see Jung, *op. cit.*, p. 210, and Abraham, Dreams and Myths, p. 22.

Now that we understand that the Fish=Child, as both are born in water, the otherwise unintelligible metaphor in the passage in Tertullian (c. 150-230 A. D.), alluded to above, becomes significant. In his work, De Baptismo, ch. 1, Tertullian, defending the rite of Christian baptism, says "Sed nos pisciculi secundum ΙΧΘΥΝ nostrum Iesum Christum in aqua nascimur, nec aliter quam in aqua permanendo solvi sumus," "But we, little fishes, even as our Ichthys, Jesus Christ, are born in water, nor can we be saved in any other way than by permanently abiding in water." The symbolism is plain. Baptism is here described as a rite of rebirth. The children, *pisciculi*, or believers, must be reborn, a symbolic idea common to classical and earlier religious conceptions, in short, a thoroughly typical case of a universal Libido analogy. This passage in Tertullian has always been regarded

---

[1] Harnack, *op. cit.* quoted by Morey.

as difficult. Naturally enough; *in aqua nascimur* relates to the *pisciculi* and to the Ἰχθύν, and it says in plain language that both are born in water, which cannot be construed into 'are baptized.' Since water as a birth symbol, was so common in antiquity (the ancients said ἡ θάλασσα, τῆς γενέσεως σύμβολον), it seems fair to infer that in the words *in aqua nascimur* Tertullian is employing traditional language, and not merely metaphorical speech, in order to carry out the figure suggested by *nos pisciculi secundum* Ἰχθύν *nostrum*. As to the second half of the passage, there may be an underlying current of thought to the effect that the believers must all remain as children. If this is so, it would be one more example of what Jung calls the typical 'infantilism' of Christian symbolic ideas.

The eucharistic significance develops out of the Christ=Fish symbolism, and is secondary from the point of view of origin. The earlier symbolism is thus found in the Aberkios epitaph and the Tertullian passage, records closely contemporaneous with the earliest occurrence of the symbol in art. The date of the symbol, that is of the absolute equivalent, Christ=Fish, may then be given as shortly after the middle of the Second Century.

The Lucina catacomb picture of the loaves and fishes may only be legitimately cited as a representation of the Multiplication. There is no reason, however, for excluding from the category of examples of the absolute Fish symbol, the Licinia Amias epitaph, for the symbolic identification of the believers with the fish, did not arise before the heathen-Christian legend of the immaculate birth of Christ ἀπὸ πηγῆς 'from the fountain.' It may indeed be the case, and Morey's arguments regarding dates seem to substantiate this view, that most of the monuments bearing simply the fish and ΙΧΘΥC, or ΙΧΘΥC alone, are later than the Second Century. These occur then just at that period when, the acrostic formula having been discovered (which must have happened about coincidently with the rise of the pictorial emblem) the symbolism attained its widest vogue. The Pektorios inscription,[1] in which the Christians are styled, Ἰχθύος οὐρανίου θεῖον γένος, "Divine race of the heavenly Fish," is an example in poetical rendering of the mystic identification of the Believers with the Saviour. The eucharistic equivalence appears also in the latter part of this inscription.

Another literary document of no less importance for our theory, though of later date, is the anonymous narrative, Ἐξήγησις τῶν πραχθέντων

---

[1] O. Pohl, Das Ichthys-Monument von Autun, 1880.

ἐν Περσίδι[1] usually cited by its Latin title, Narratio rerum quae in Perside acciderunt. This remarkable document in which heathen-Asiatic and Christian elements are mingled, belongs probably to the Fifth Century. The part concerning the fish symbolism is found in a story which critics agree goes back to an earlier source, placed by the writer in the mouth of one of his characters. The narrative tells us: "King Cyrus built a magnificent temple to Hera, and set up in it gold and silver images of the gods. Once the king came to the temple to receive the interpretation of his dreams, and was greeted by the priest with the announcement that Hera was with child. In answer to the king's demand for an explanation, the priest described the wondrous occurrences of the night before, how the images of the gods danced together, celebrating the pregnancy of Hera. Even as he finished his narrative, the roof of the temple opened and a star stood above the statue of Hera, whom they called now Hera, now the Fountain (πηγή) and again Myria; and a voice prophesied the immaculate birth from her of a child that should be the Beginning and the End " . . . [Morey]. Throughout the narrative, Hera, the Fountain, is identified with Mary, and in the praises of her which the priest puts into the mouths of the images, the following explanation of the Fountain is given: " For the Fountain of water flows ever with the water of the spirit, having the one and only fish, taken with the hook of divinity, which feeds the whole world, as if dwelling in the sea, with its own flesh " [Morey]. Identical imagery with that of the Aberkios inscription — the Fish *caught* by the *hook* of divinity *in the water*, Fountain, πηγή=Mary[2] (Fish=child symbolism), and the feeding of the whole world with its flesh (eucharistic symbolism).

In conclusion it is interesting to note that the symbolic language of this narrative, whose pagan-Christian character is only too evident, is regarded by Morey as not reflecting purely subjective fancy, or personal invention of the writer, but as reminiscent of imagery which had long been traditional. It is curious that the underlying meaning of the

[1] E. Bratke, Das sogenannte Religionsgespräch am Hof der Sasaniden, Texte und Untersuchungen, N. F. Bd. 4, 3 Heft.

[2] A mediaeval altar-piece in Brunswick (Evans, Animal Symbolism in Ecclesiastical Architecture, p. 25), bears a representation of the Virgin seated with a unicorn resting its head in her lap. This and many other mediaeval pictures illustrate the symbolism of immaculate conception by the unicorn's horn (a phallic emblem). On the Brunswick triptych is the inscription near the Virgin FONS SIGNATUS, ' Sealed fountain,' a plain allusion to the same concept as contained in the Narratio, i. e. Virgo=Fons. The same symbolic language is found in The Song of Solomon, ch. IV, 12, " A garden enclosed (literally *barred*) is my sister, my spouse ; *a spring shut up, a fountain sealed.*"

symbolism was not at once perceived from the correspondence of the story found both in the Aberkios inscription and this narrative. But the principle of generic symbolism existing as the common property of mankind, and appearing in different ages, was more or less unknown to us. Religious conservatism too operated in rejecting or obscuring such pagan traits as the analogy of the Virgin and the fountain nymph, and the miraculous birth of Christ in accordance with the traditional pagan account of the Myth of the Birth of the Hero.[1]

THE SWASTIKA, THE TRISKELES (LYCIAN SYMBOL, SICILIAN SYMBOL, ETC.), THE ANKH AND THE WINGED DISK

From the foregoing it will have been understood that the word, symbol, is here used, not as in numismatic terminology, to denote an accessory sign or device on a coin, subordinate to the type proper, but in the ordinary sense of the word, as a token ($\sigma\dot{\upsilon}\mu\beta o\lambda o\nu$) or representation of an idea or concept. A symbol may be defined as a concrete picture or emblem which evokes an image or concept by means of an analogue rather than by an exact reproduction. The symbol is therefore a substitute or surrogate, that is, it stands for something else; and there is usually some point of resemblance between the sign and the thing signified. According to common usage, all signs are called symbols, but in a more restricted sense, the sign as a representative image or picture is not a symbol, whereas it is one when employed in an analogous way. The ideographic signs in the Egyptian writing-system will serve to illustrate this point about the two uses of the graphic symbol. The circle with central dot has its representative or pictographic value as ' sun.' It also stands for ' light, day, divisions of time,' etc., and with this ideographic value it becomes a true symbol. The sign of a vase full of grain, or pouring out grain, means representatively ' cereals,' but symbolically ' harvest, tribute.' Among the hieroglyphics used in modern astronomical works we may discriminate in the same

---

[1] O. Rank, Der Mythus von der Geburt des Helden, cited above, makes a study of the peculiar circumstances attending the Hero's Advent, according to myth, a most instructive chapter in comparative mythology. In view of Rank's investigations, it would seem rather idle to discuss at the present day such questions as " The Virgin Birth in the Second Century," Princeton Theological Review, 1912, from the point of view as to whether it was based on fact or legend.

way, on the one hand, between the sign, crescent, for 'moon,' and the sign, circle with enclosed cross (the four points of the compass), for 'earth,' which are both patent designs, simple pictures of reality, and on the other hand, the signs for Aries, Taurus, Gemini, Leo, etc., which are graphic shorthand for the symbolic concepts under which these zodiacal constellations were imagined. When we attempt to inquire into their ultimate derivation, we are face to face with the problem of ancient astronomical symbolism. So, when in myth and symbol-picture the sun is conceived as a bull and the moon as a cow, the similitude is not immediately obvious, for we have here to deal with a disguised analogy.

The problem of interpreting symbols is the determination of the laws of association or analogy. Why was the peacock in Christian symbolism the emblem of immortality? Why do the serpent and sphinx figure on classical tomb-stones? What is the meaning of the fabulous phoenix? What do the fantastic animal figures of early religions (and Christian) signify? Whence came the caduceus of Hermes and the thyrsos of Dionysos? Answers to many of these and similar questions have been given, some of which are partially satisfactory explanations. But it may be said that until the psychological roots of symbolism were known, until the essence of symbolism was discovered in unconscious phantasy, no general analysis of symbol and myth had been formulated which synthesized the whole subject under a broad principle proved valid by the test of the workings of the individual- and the mass-soul.

As shown in our introduction, mythology is a creation of the human psyche whose origin is traceable to the unconscious primitive and infantile. In the language of psychoanalysis, the adaptation of the individual and the race to the real world is accompanied by a conflict between the pleasure and reality principles. The unconscious is anti-social, and would proceed towards its end without disguise of the driving impulse. But it meets with obstacles perceived by our conscious personalities as social and desirable. This impulse must consequently be sublimated. Though repressed, it nevertheless demands expression. The prohibited could be allowed to the super-beings, the gods, and the conflict thus solved. This sublimation we see in the case of Taboos and other prohibitions which were even enjoined upon priests as a religious duty. Thus the human emotional conflict was solved by the gratification in phantasy. "This function of admission and symbolically dressed gratification of socially inapplicable instinctive impulses, the myth shares with religion with which it long formed an insepar-able unit."[1]

Starting with this viewpoint we shall discuss symbolism, whether as pictorial image or myth, on Greek coins. Any type or emblem on a Greek coin, not a simple genre object or scene from everyday life, or a portrait head, may be included, provided it has a symbolic connotation. Even portrait heads, if heroized or deified, would fall within our cate-gory. There are many of these symbols which are readily understood, especially those whose association is regular and whose implication is not far below the surface. Others again, while understood in their common import, have to be analyzed more profoundly when the ordi-nary interpretation does not seem to suit the particular case. The practical aim which we have set before us is to throw new light on certain of the less-understood symbols and mythical presentations with reference to the Libido theory of their origin.

THE SWASTIKA — BIBLIOGRAPHY

The swastika is a symbol of such great antiquity, first appearing on objects belonging to the Third Millenium B. C., and of such uni-versal and prolonged use, being found in the Old and New Worlds, and employed as a living symbol to this day in China, Japan, Tibet and India, that its origin and meaning have naturally excited the greatest curiosity. A voluminous literature has grown up about the subject, in which there will not be found any general accord on the moot points of its genesis and significance. The monograph devoted to the subject by T. R. Wilson, The Swastika, in the Report of the Smithsonian Institution, Washington, D. C., 1896, is a very complete summary of all that had been written on the symbol to date. No special thesis in regard to the meaning is there advocated, and no particular home-place, assuming a monogenist or single-source origin, is determined. An extensive bib-liography is given at the end of Wilson's work, to which may now be added the following:

A. R. Hein, Mäander, Kreuze, Hakenkreuze etc. in Amerika, Vienna, 1891.

A. Bertrand, Le Swastika ou Croix gammée, Nos Origines, La Religion des Gau-lois, Paris, 1897.

M. Zmigrodski, Correspondenz-Blatt der deutschen Gesellschaft für Anthropolo-gie etc., XXVIII, no. 3, 1897, p. 165.

[1] Otto Rank and Hanns Sachs, The Significance of Psychoanalysis for the Mental Sciences, The Psychoanalytic Review, 1916, p. 76.

Mrs. Z. Nuttall, The Fundamental Principles of Old and New World Civilizations, Archaeological and Ethnological Papers of the Peabody Museum, Cambridge, Mass., vol. II, 1901.

W. Wallace Tooker, The Swastika and Other Marks among the Eastern Algonquins, The American Antiquarian, Dec., 1898.

L. de Milloué, Le Svastika, Annales du Musée Guimet, vol. 31, 1909.

References of importance are also to be found in the following publications:

J. Déchelette, Manuel d'Archéologie préhistorique, II, Paris, 1910, pp. 453 ff.

W. Schultz, Das Hakenkreuz als Grundzeichen des westsemitischen Alphabets, Memnon, 1909, III, pp. 175 ff.

A. B. Cook, Zeus, A Study in Ancient Religion, Cambridge, Eng., 1914.

G. and A. de Mortillet, Musée Préhistorique, 2nd edit., Paris, 1903.

R. Dussaud, Les Civilisations préhelléniques dans le bassin de la Mer Égée, Paris, 1914.

A. Mosso, The Dawn of Mediterranean Civilization, London, 1910.

W. Dörpfeld, Troja und Ilion, Athens, 1902, Vol. I. Anhang, Die thönernen Spinnwirtel by Hubert Schmidt. Id. Zeitschrift für Ethnologie, 1903, Tordos, p. 457 ff.

There is no article s. v. Swastika in the Encyclopedia Brittanica, Eleventh Edition, 1910, and under the word 'Cross,' there is a superficial, inaccurate statement regarding the symbol. The New International Encyclopedia, New York, 1908, gives a brief and fairly accurate account derived mainly from Wilson. This article is the most accessible for quick reference, but Déchelette's discussion is the best for thorough orientation in the subject. His treatment is up to date on the historical side, and sane in theory. The bibliography of the swastika on coins is given by R. Mowat in the Bull. de la Soc. des Ant. de France, 1896, p. 239. Numismatists will however most readily turn to the two articles in the Numismatic Chronicle, 1880, by E. Thomas, The Indian Swastika and its Western Counterparts, and by P. Gardner, Ares as a Sun-God, etc. The article by L. Müller, Det Saakaldte Hagekors, Kongeligt Dansk Videnskabernes Selskab, Bind 5, no. 1, Copenhagen, 1877, contains references to coins. This part of the subject has nowhere been thoroughly treated.

DIFFERENT FORMS OF THE SIGN

The swastika, or, as it is called, the gammated cross (croix gammée), hook-cross (Hakenkreuz), is a sign which may be described as an equal-armed cross having ends bent at right angles to the four limbs, and all in one direction, right or left, Fig. B, 1, 2. It has been likened to a composite figure made of Greek 'gammas.' This simple form is the original one, and though various by-forms of the original

Fig. B.

figure are found, as well as numerous swastika-like compositions, the primitive type has persisted to our day.[1] There are so many of these adaptations of the simple type that it would be impossible to cite them all here. One may consult the illustrations in the three chief sources, Wilson, Bertrand and Goblet d'Alviella, The Migration of Symbols, London, 1894. The arms of the swastika are sometimes curved instead of straight, a by-form which was very early developed, Fig. B, 3, and this form occasionally has the curving arms twisted into a spiral, Fig. B, 4. Since the curvilinear forms are found on the Trojan spindle whorls, Figs. 5, 6, 9, sometimes on the same whorl with the rectilinear swastika (cf. Wilson, Figs. 57, 66, 78), they are doubtless mere varieties. The sign on Indian coins often takes this curving form, Pl. XVI, 27, 29, 30. Another modification is seen in Fig. B, 5, where the bent ends of the 'cross' are continued in one or more lines, each at right angles to the preceding. This form is very commonly found in company with the simpler type on Greek vases of the Geometric Period, Figs. 23-25. The swastika somewhat rarely has four points or dots in the angles of intersection of the cross-lines, Fig. B, 6. An example of this type is Fig. 16, a pottery fragment from Thera of considerable antiquity. It occurs also on the Trojan whorls (Schliemann, Atlas, 2982), and on a 'late Mycenean' vase from Melos, Fig. 15, and on a gold-leaf ornament from Mycenae.[2] Curiously enough this rarer and very ancient variety is seen on a modern commercial trade-mark from Denmark, Fig. 17.

There are also a great many swastika-like figures (cf. Bertrand, Wilson, etc.). The tetraskeles, which is very like the curvilinear

[1] This illustrates the generalization that ornamental motives are conservative, and tend to survive in the same form rather than in new combinations. On the Greek Geometric vases the swastika is treated as a purely decorative ornament and undergoes modification of its early shape. Yet the original form is found side by side with the modified one, and recurs on Greek vases of a much later period, Figs. 30-32, where it is used as a symbol.

[2] Wilson, *op. cit.*, Fig. 161. Compare also the early electrum coin shown below in Fig. 43.

swastika, though the arms are more nearly crescent-shaped than on the latter, and do not intersect,[1] but are attached to a central circle or boss, is a variety of the triskeles, or Lycian symbol, which will be discussed separately. Then there is the swastika-like Labyrinth on the coins of Knossos (see below), a form which is possibly of significance in connection with the original meaning of the Labyrinth (Cook, *op. cit.*, pp. 476ff.). There are arrangements of animal figures into swastika combinations on the coins of Gaul, of horses, etc. (Bertrand, *op. cit.*, fig. 13; Goblet d'Alviella, Pl. II, 14). In Crete there was found a very early clay seal-impression with double axes arranged into a swastika composition, Fig. 12. On a coin of India the ends of the swastika are terminated by the ' taurine ' symbol Pl. XVI, 36. In fact the swastika composition is found in many forms and in many places. In India there is a plan of a village known as ' the swastika,'[2] which, though, it bears actually only a slight resemblance to the figure, is considered to be derived from that of a military camp. Of course it would be natural for the people of India who still regard the symbol with reverence as a magic sign, to see the swastika figure in all manner of designs, so that reliance may reasonably be placed upon this statement. The posture of the Buddha statues seated *à la Turque* with arms crossed over the breasts is known as ' the swastika '.[3] Finally the Jain sect is said to make the sign of the swastika when entering a temple as Catholics make the sign of the cross.[4] Much mystic symbolism is attached by the Indian people of the present time to all the ancient signs (and they are legion) in their religion and art, indeed, to such an extent that the mystico-philosophical meanings nearly obscure the original sense.

ANTIQUITY AND PLACE OF ORIGIN OF THE SWASTIKA

GENERAL CONSIDERATIONS

Since the appearance of Wilson's article with its wealth of citation and illustration, it might seem that there was little left to say, not enough perhaps, to justify an entirely fresh discussion. Wilson's work will remain for a long time the classical reference for the monuments

---

[1] That is, in the original figure as first known to us on Lycian coins.

[2] E. B. Havell, The Ancient and Mediaeval Architecture of India : a Study of Indo-Aryan Civilization, London, 1915, p. 17, fig. 5.

[3] Wilson, *op. cit.* p. 882.

[4] Ib. p. 804. Note also, on p. 803, the testimony as to the popular use of the swastika in modern India.

and for summaries of opinion up to date. But, since Wilson wrote, the chronology of the prehistoric antiquities of the Bronze and Iron Age civilizations of Europe, Western Asia and the Mediterranean has been put upon a scientific basis. In particular, Montelius' great work in systematizing the chronology of the various epochs of the Bronze Age in Italy[1] has given us a point of support without which we might still hesitate to open again the problem of the historical origin of the swastika. For example, it need no longer be held with Goodyear[2] that the first-known specimen of the swastika occurs on a hut urn from Central Italy, Fig. 26. Hut urns of this type are dated by Montelius in Bronze Age IV (of Italy) c. 1200 B. C.,[3] that is just at the threshold of the Iron Age. The swastika on the well-known Trojan spindle whorls, Figs. 4-9, are much earlier. Also the example impressed on a fragment of pottery found with the punch itself in the lacustrine station at Lac du Bourget, Savoy (Wilson, Figs. 195, 196), can not be cited as one of the oldest occurrences,[4] for excellent authorities concur in dating these objects in the later Bronze or early Iron Age.[5]

Furthermore, the great discoveries in Crete and Melos which revolutionized all our ideas of prehistoric Mediterranean civilization were not begun until 1900, four years after Wilson wrote. There are additions to the prehistoric swastikas to be made from these finds. The valuable chronological system, erected upon a solid basis by Evans and other archaeologists, has furnished a series of scientifically supported periods within which to classify by approximate dates the monuments of pre-Hellenic civilization in the Aegean. Cretan, or as it is called, Minoan chronology has had the effect of establishing a more exact dating of the Trojan finds.

We shall now discuss the origin of the symbol historically and show its geographical distribution, and leave the question of its significance for subsequent consideration. Neither Chaldaea (Babylonia and Assyria), nor ancient Egypt, nor Phoenicia employed the sign. In

[1] O. Montelius, La Civilization Primitive en Italie, Stockholm, 1895–1910.

[2] W. H. Goodyear, The Grammar of the Lotus, pp. 348ff.

[3] Montelius, *op. cit.* Pl. 140. 9 (Latium).

[4] L. de Milloué, Le Svastika, *op. cit.*, p. 91, " En Suisse on l'a trouvé assez fréquemment dans les habitations lacustres, ou palafittes, avec des objets de la fin de l'époque de la pierre polie et du premier âge du bronze."

[5] Bertrand, *op. cit.*, p. 143. Déchelette, *op. cit.*, II, p. 456. The two instances here cited are, moreover, very doubtful examples of the swastika; the one, Fig. 26, looks more like a fragment of the maeander pattern, the other (Bertrand, *op. cit.*, Fig. 6) is a very uncertain case (cf. below).

China and India the swastika is not found until a period which in comparison with prehistory is relatively late. The name by which the symbol is known to us, is a Sanskrit word used by Aryan Indians, but the symbol itself is not of ancient date in India. The popular modern idea, still widely current, that India is the home-place of the swastika is erroneous. The Indian examples are not much older than c. 350 B. C.,[1] a date which we may think of as modern in contrast to the Third Millenium, when the symbol is found at ancient Troy.

Wilson states on the authority of Goblet d'Alviella that the swastika was found on a Hittite bas-relief cut in the rock at Ibrîz, ancient Kybistra, Cappadocia. Upon examining the reproduction of this rock sculpture,[2] we find a meander-like border running along the border of the robe of a king or priest. This border is not of the continuous fret pattern, but a succession of swastika designs enclosed in squares. This is therefore no true example of a swastika used as symbol. When the sign is used as a symbol on human or divine figures it is in the form of an independent device placed upon some part of the body or garment. The Ibrîz sculptured relief is moreover of no great antiquity, its date being about 900 B. C.[3] Since by that time both swastika and maeander had long been in common use in Greek art, this is probably a case of ' migration '. It is valueless in tracing the original home of the sign, since other Hittite monuments do not show it. Schliemann stated that the symbol had been seen on a Hittite cylinder,[4] but this is apparently not confirmed.

The next case which we shall consider is that of certain pottery marks in the form of the swastika occurring on sherds from Kahun, Egypt. Goodyear states that " The earliest swastikas are of the Third Millenium B. C., and occur on foreign Cyprian and Carian (?) pottery fragments of the time of the twelfth dynasty (in Egypt), discovered by Mr. Flinders Petrie in 1889 ".[5] The fragments in question bear scratched

---

[1] The word ' swastika ' occurs in the grammar of Pāṇini, c. 350 B. C. On Indian coins the symbol cannot be demonstrated as occurring any earlier, but it is probable that the symbol was in use some time previous to the time of Pāṇini, when the word was incorporated in the grammar as an integral part of the Sanskrit language; and, as the name of a particular sign, not merely as a term for ' well-being ' the meaning of ' swastika ' according to derivation. We may therefore assign 500 B. C. as a conjectural earliest date for the symbol in India (cf. Bertrand's discussion, *op. cit.* pp. 176ff.).

[2] Perrot et Chipiez, Histoire de l'Art dans l'Antiquité, vol. IV, pp. 724ff., Fig. 354.

[3] J. Garstang, The Land of the Hittites, London, 1910, pp. 191ff.

[4] Schliemann, Troja, p. 125.

[5] Grammar of the Lotus, p. 356.

potter's marks incised in the clay before firing, on a ware not described by Petrie,[1] and assumed by Goodyear to be Cypriote or 'Carian.' They were unearthed at Kahun among deposits of the Twelfth Egyptian Dynasty (central date c. 2000 B. C.).[2] Similar incised marks are found on pottery at different places in the Mediterranean region, and have been regarded as indicating an early linear script. The whole matter is still quite obscure. It is said that an incised swastika mark has been found on Neolithic pottery from Tordos in Transylvania.[3] The evidence is very scanty, and not enough to prove that the swastika was a primitive writing-sign, though there would be no surprise if this should be established. If it belonged to a whole stock of inherited signs from which later scripts were derived, we may expect to see it at any place where prehistoric commerce carried the writing system. It is a tempting hypothesis thus to account for the contemporaneous appearance of the swastika symbol at Troy and in the island of Melos (cf. below), for the art of Northern Asia Minor was quite dissimilar to that of the Aegean, and it is hard to account otherwise for the appearance of the swastika at the same time in these two centres of distinct cultures. If it should be proved that the swastika symbol was a character of a prehistoric script, the case would be analogous to that of the Ankh symbol which was an Egyptian hieroglyph. It is not found however in the Minoan linear script, though Mosso states that it is among the signs occurring on stone blocks in the palace at Phaistos.[4] Schmidt, *op. cit.*, regards the swastikas on the Trojan whorls, and also a group of isolated signs common to the whorls and (as incised marks) to the pottery of Tordos and Kahun as possible writing signs. Evans, *op. cit.*, p. 6, refers to the writing-like signs of Troy (including presumably the swastika) as the 'rude graffiti of Hissarlik,' and adds " So far as they may be regarded as signs, it seems safest to interpret these rude linear figures in the Neolithic and Early Metal Age pottery of Hissarlik and Broos (i. e. *Tordos*) as simple ideographs rather than as syllables or letters." Some of the marks on the whorls suggest a writing system, and it is possible that some of them may be so regarded. The objection to this assumption is of course the lack of any monument on which the signs

[1] A. J. Evans, Scripta Minoa, Oxford, 1909, p. 2, writes " It must, however, be observed that those (i. e. *marks*) found at Gurob and in the still earlier settlement at Kahun, were in no single instance incised on pottery that can, in any probability, be regarded as of Aegean fabric."

[2] Flinders Petrie, Kahun, Gurob and Hawara, Pl. 27, figs. 161, 162.

[3] H. Schmidt, Zeitschrift für Ethnologie, 1903, p. 459.

[4] *Op. cit.*, p. 35.

are found combined in a series which looks like writing, and, for the swastika, the fact that it is actually seen in repetitions all over the whorls. The evidence as to these isolated marks found at Kahun, Troy, Tordos and in the Aegean being signs of a common writing system is far from conclusive. At all events we shall later see reason for believing that the swastika at Troy had already acquired the value of a symbol, whatever its origin in more remote times.

Quite recently the swastika has been found on a pottery fragment, Fig. C, from Elam, or Susiana, as modern geographers designate that district of Persia which was occupied by an ancient civilization probably anterior to Babylonian culture. The sherd came from the Tepé Moussian near Susa,[1] in which were discovered objects for which a date as early as the Neolithic age is claimed. Some objects of metal in copper and bronze were found, and also hatchets of polished stone. The pottery, terracottas, spindle whorls, etc., seem very ancient. J. de Morgan assigns the sepultures of Moussian to the end of the Fifth Millenium.[2] Other archaeologists have criticized the dates given by de Morgan for Elamite civilization as to early by a millenium or so. On the whole it would be safer to regard this fragment as belonging to the Bronze Age. Its interest lies chiefly in the place where it was found. In a different work,[3] de Morgan said that he had never encountered the symbol in Elam, and that ' it apparently entered the ancient world at the same time as the Aryans and Europeans '. The evidence in general favors this presumption, though we need not express it in this way. We should rather say that the swastika is, in the earliest period, co-extensive with the Bronze Age civilization of the Mediterranean basin. But we need not involve the problem of origin with the race question by assuming any theory of prehistoric migration, as, for example, from a South-central European home-place.[4] All that our present knowledge leads us to believe is that the sign was indigenous

<hr>

[1] J. E. Gautier et G. Lempre, Memoires de la Délegation en Perse, 1905, p. 110, Fig. 176.

[2] J. de Morgan, Les Dernières Fouilles de Susiane, Revue de l'Art Ancien et Moderne, 1908, p. 409.

[3] Id. Les Premières Civilisations, Paris, 1909, p. 169, note 2.

[4] Underlying many statements or conjectures about the primitive center of diffusion of the symbol is the implication that it is ' Aryan,' and therefore a ' migration ' from South-Central Europe, southwards, is commonly predicated. The actual evidence for the existence of the swastika in Bronze Age settlements in South-Central Europe seems to go back to the rare examples on the hut-urn from Latium and the matrix and vase fragment from Savoy, discussed above, neither of which has very strong claim to pass as a swastika. The rest of the antiquities from South Central Europe bearing the sign, cited by Wilson and others, do not date before the Iron Age.

to Mediterranean lands, for with the present exception of Elam, it does not occur in the earliest period outside that area. We can only record this example, and await further knowledge of the little-known Elamite culture.

The following examples, Figs. D, E, are from the Mediterranean region, but may best be classed apart from the main series. The one

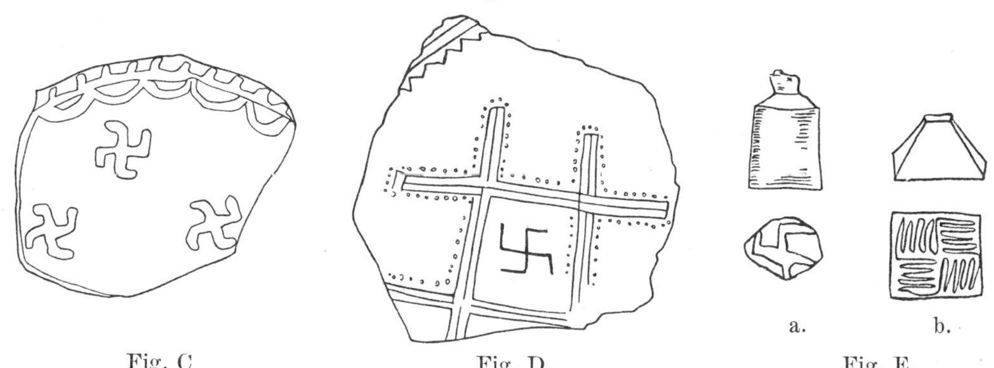

Fig. C   Fig. D.   a.   b.   Fig. E.

illustrated in Fig. D (Mosso, *op. cit.*, p. 263, Fig. 15) is a sherd from southern Italy of uncertain date. The settlement from which it came is said by Mosso to be possibly Neolithic, but no reliable chronological data is forthcoming. Fig. E, a, b, shows two so-called 'pintaderas,' or tatooing stamps, which were found at Hagia Triada in eastern Crete (Mosso, *op. cit.*, p. 258, Fig. 149C, D). For these objects on which are (a) a swastika, and (b) a possible swastika design, a Neolithic date is claimed. These swastikas would then be even earlier than our earliest Trojan examples (Fig. 1, c. 2500-2000 B. C.) since the introduction of metal in Crete is placed at about 2800 B. C. However we have not included them in our descriptive list, as their date is somewhat conjectural and the evidence fragmentary. If admitted as examples of the sign, these 'pintaderas' and the pottery marks on vase-fragments from Kahun, Tordos, etc., would carry back the swastika to a more hoary antiquity than heretofore predicated. But all the examples here under consideration are not of a character to carry much conviction in a scientific argument.

MONUMENTS BEARING THE SWASTIKA

I. The Earliest Swastikas. Troy, Crete and Melos. The Bronze Age, c. 3000-1200 B. C.

The earliest specimen of the swastika which can be reliably dated is the one occurring on a fragment of black incised ware with white filling, Fig. 1,[1] found in the lowest stratum at Hissarlik, Troy I, c. 3000-2500 B. C. Schliemann at first attributed this sherd to the First City, or lowest settlement of the hill of Hissarlik, but later he concluded that it had really come from the Third City (Ilios, p. 350, n 1). In the new publication of Schliemann's excavations, however, the piece is assigned to the First City[2] in accordance with a scientific classification of the pottery, whorls, etc., on the basis of fabric. The next example comes from the Second City, Troy II, c. 2500-2000 B. C., and occurs on one of the famous 'Owl' vases, or human-shaped vases, Fig. 2,[3] so characteristic of primitive art. Here the sign is found on the navel (or vulva ?) of a vase with human attributes, eyes, nose, mouth and breasts. In Fig. 3,[4] is represented another vase of the same class, having a cross with four points as ornament in the same position. This latter design, called the cross cantonnée is a common motif in primitive Greek art, and may have had a symbolic significance. Whether it is related to the swastika or not will be debated later. The position on which these signs are placed, on the idol-like vases, navel or vulva, certainly leads us to suppose that they had some significance beyond that of mere ornaments. In view of the undoubted existence of the

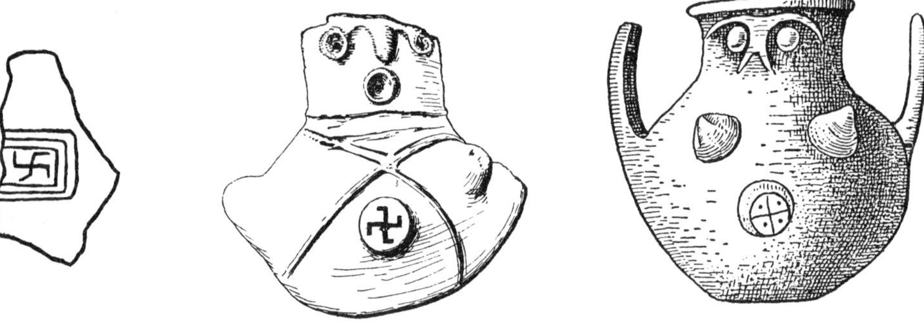

Fig. 1.   Fig. 2.   Fig. 3.

swastika on what is more probably the vulva of the vase, Fig. 2, it really seems rather questionable that the lead statuette[5] found also at Hissarlik, Troy III, should now be said to have no swastika incised on the triangular shaped vulva. The Berlin authorities inform us that, after the cleaning, the swastika, which Schliemann saw and recorded, and which is clearly seen in his reproduction of the figure, has disappeared,[6] a circumstance taken to prove that it was an illusory sort of thing, a figment on the part of Schliemann. Sayce also believed that

---

[1] Schliemann, Ilios, Fig. 247.   [2] Dörpfeld, *op. cit.*, I, p. 252.   [3] Schliemann Troja, Fig. 101.
[4] Id. Ilios, Fig. 869.   [5] Id. Ilios, Fig. 126 = Wilson, *op. cit.*, Fig. 125.
[6] Memnon III, Pl. II. 16 and p. 193, note 2.

there was a swastika on the lead idol,[1] so that we have to conclude that his eyes also deceived him. The affair seems somewhat mysterious, and one would like further information as to the appearance of the idol before cleaning, from those who examined it in Berlin and superintended the work, before deciding finally against Schliemann.

The next examples occur on spindle whorls and clay disks all coming from the village settlements lying between the stratum known as the Burnt City, Troy II and the Sixth or Homeric (Mycenean) City, usually grouped as Troy III-V, c. 2000-1500 B. C. Only a few specimens are here figured. Fig. 4[2] has four swastikas symmetrically arranged, and of ordinary form. In Fig. 5[3] is seen a biconical spindle whorl ornamented with concentric circles and a curvilinear swastika superimposed upon a circle. Figs. 60, 64, 65, 69 and 70 in Wilson's work show a similar ornamentation with one swastika (Fig. 60 with

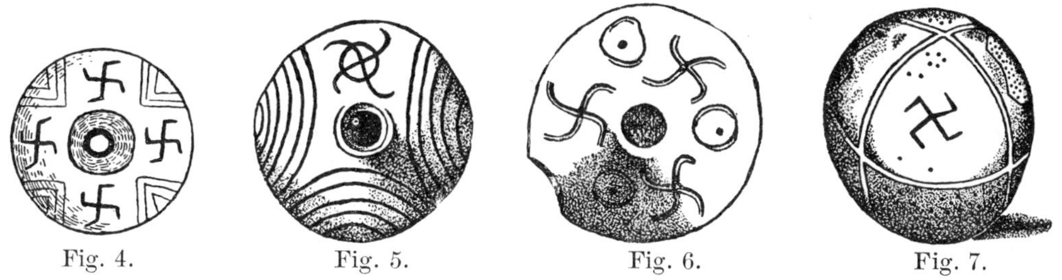

Fig. 4. Fig. 5. Fig. 6. Fig. 7.

two) of the usual form, so that there is no doubt that the form in Fig. 5 is a swastika. The following, Fig. 6,[4] also with swastikas somewhat curvilinear alternating with a circle or disk with central dot, shows plainly enough how the variety in Fig. 5 arose. The next illustration,

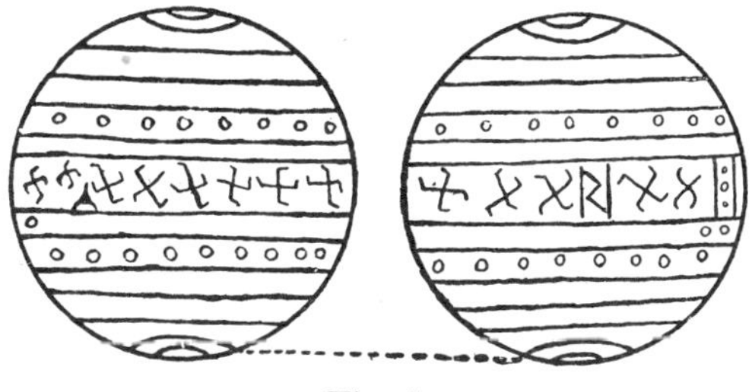

Fig. 8.

Fig. 7,[5] is a clay ball with decoration of lines dividing the surface into segments, in one of which is a swastika, while one of the others contains what looks like a tree. Fig. 8[6] gives two drawings showing the

[1] Ilios, p. 353.
[2] De Mortillet, *op. cit.*, Fig. 1240; Schliemann, Atlas Trojanischer Alterthümer, Fig. 2971.
[3] Ilios, Fig. 1987.   [4] Ib. Fig. 1990.   [5] Ib. Fig. 1999.   [6] Ib. Figs. 245, 246.

entire surface of a clay ball on which are parallel lines, latitudinal, and a band of thirteen swastikas with division marks separating two from the rest. That there was any special meaning attached to the number thirteen here, it would seem rather rash to affirm, but the presence of the sign as an exclusive device on this clay sphere, and as an isolated mark on the one shown in Fig. 7 (and others, cf. Wilson, Fig. 76) seems evidence enough taken in connection with the example in Fig. 2 and its later history, to prove that the sign had at this time a symbolic value. Next comes a whorl, Fig. 9,[1] shown in two views with the curvilinear form of the sign with spiral ends. Fig. 10[2] is a design from a whorl consisting of a circle with arms extending from it similar to the arms of the swastika, and disks with a point interspersed between these arms. Designs generally similar are to be seen in Wilson, Figs. 88 and 90. The circle with swastika-like arms suggests a rotating solar disk, especially when associated with circles with central point, a common primitive representation of the sun. A bronze fibula, Fig. 27, shows similar bent arms on the periphery of a circle, evidently part of a sun picture. Full discussion of the original significance of the swastika is deferred, however, until all examples have been examined, and the distribution of the symbol and its modern meaning have been considered.

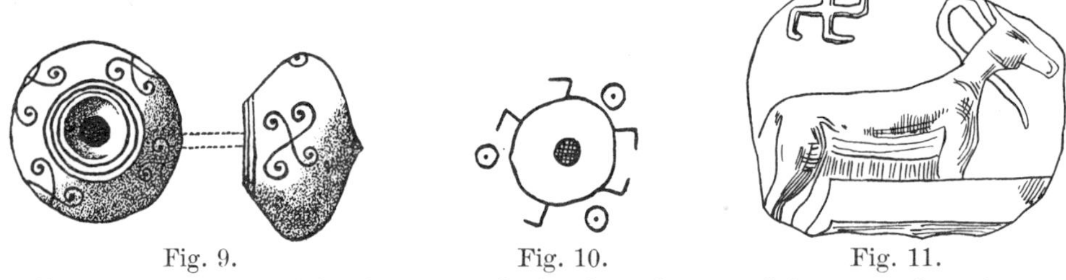

Fig. 9.   Fig. 10.   Fig. 11.

Contemporary with the whorls is the clay seal impression from the Temple Repositories at Knossos, Crete, Fig. 11.[3] This impressed sealing (with eighteen others) was found by Evans among objects which he dates in Middle Minoan III, c. 1900-1700 B. C. It represents a Cretan wild goat standing near a trough (?), and in the field above is a swastika. The goat figures in Cretan or Minoan religion, and while we should not care to go so far, even in speculation, as the great master of Aegean archaeology, Evans, has gone in connecting the sign as a sacred emblem with Zeus, still the next example brings further conviction

[1] Ib. Fig. 1868.   [2] Ib. Fig. 1951.
[3] Annual of the British School at Athens, IX (1902–3), p. 88, Fig. 59.

that the Minoans used the sign with sacred intent. This is a clay seal-ing also from the same Knossian site, Fig. 12,[1] on which the double axe, a potent symbol in Minoan religion, is arranged fourfold into a swastika composition. If any sceptic had asked to be shown examples from the prehistoric period in which the sign occurred with indubitable sacred

Fig. 12.   Fig. 13.   Fig. 14.

meaning, we could do no better than this, unless indeed it could be shown upon an altar or employed in a certain religious scene. Sceptics used to feel the same way about the double axe and its religious signifi-cance until convinced by the ever-increasing number of examples showing more and more clearly the sacred significance of the sign, which besides being a sacred symbol, was employed as a mason's mark

Fig. 15.

on stone blocks in the Knossian palace, and as an ideographic sign in Minoan script. It was not necessary to demand to be shown the dou-ble axe posed on what could with certainty be identified as an altar, after seeing its occurrence in religious scenes on rings. So too the

---

[1] R. von Lichtenberg, Die Ägäische Kultur, Leipzig, 1911, Fig. 68.

swastika on the sealing with the goat will be convincing to all but the super-sceptical.

The next examples are important as showing the continuance of the use of the sign on pottery. They are (1) fragments of pre-Mycenean Geometric ware from the island of Melos, Figs. 13, 14,[1] found in the excavations at Phylakopi, and contemporary with the spindle whorls and Knossian sealings, belonging to the period known as Phylakopi II, c. 1900-1500 B. C. ; and (2) a vase, Fig. 15,[2] of local Mycenean fabric, Phylakopi III, 1500-1200 B. C., with flower designs, and swastikas with four dots, curvilinear, scattered amid the naturalistic designs. There are other examples of the sign from Melos on pottery objects of the same period. These latter instances are particularly interesting as forming the connecting link with the pottery of the Iron Age in Greece. The example of a clay disk from Thera, Fig. 16,[3] is

Fig. 16.

given here for comparison with the swastikas on Fig. 15. It has a unique interest on account of the four dots in the angles of the intersecting limbs (cf. also Fig. 3 above). The swastika curvilinear, with four dots is found also on early electrum coins, Uncertain Ionian class, B. M. C. Ionia, Pl. II. 20, and our coin list no. 2, Fig. 43. The modern trade-mark for Danish beer of Ny Carlsberg, Fig. 17,[4] contains

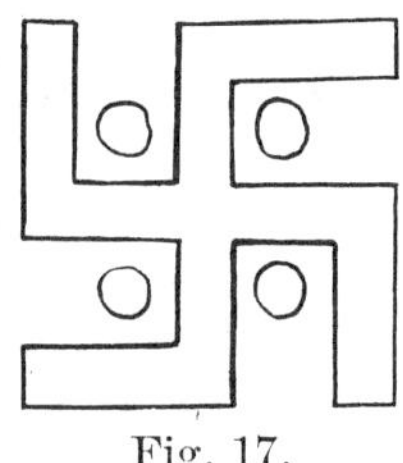

Fig. 17.

a peculiar feature for a modern swastika, namely the surprising survival of the four dots,[5] a detail which could perhaps be traced to a prototype among European swastikas,[6] unless of course it was copied out

---

[1] Journal of Hellenic Studies, Sup. Paper, No 4, Excavations at Phylakopi in Melos, Pls. XII. 9, XIII. 3.

[2] Ibid, Fig. 97.

[3] J. B. Waring, Ceramic Art in Remote Ages, etc., London, 1874, Pl. 42. 2.

[4] Hein, *op. cit.*, Fig. 10. [5] See above, p. 117.

[6] E. g. through survival from the Hallstatt period, cf. Fig. 28.

of some book on the symbol in which this Theran example was figured, but this seems less probable.

II. The Swastika on Greek Pottery. The Iron Age in Greece, c. 1200-500 B. C.

Goodyear made the sound observation that the true home of the swastika is to be found in the pottery of the Greek Geometric style, since there it is found in largest dimension.[1] His theory was that while the symbol might have been employed in an earlier and 'imperfect' form on the hut urn of Italy (cf. Fig. 26), its real centre of diffusion was in the pottery of the Geometric (Iron) Age from the islands of Cyprus, Rhodes and Melos, etc., and from the Greek mainland. This view the above discussion of examples from the Bronze Age period in Crete and Melos (unknown when Goodyear wrote) shows to be substantially correct. Before the discovery of these swastikas from the very heart and centre of prehistoric Greek culture, the oldest known home of the sign in Greece was Troy, and it was a natural supposition to look to South Central Europe as the pre-Trojan home of the symbol, especially as the former hypothesis of an 'Aryan' migration from this locality into Greek lands supported this view. But no examples from South Central Europe[2] go back to anything like the remote epoch of the Cretan seal-impression and the pre-Mycenean Geometric fragments of Melos. Furthermore, the modern view presupposes for the Aegean area an autocthonous population, the Mediterranean race, to whom the oldest European civilization is due.[3] The swastika belongs to the Third Millenium of prehistoric Greece, and there is no evidence to establish an earlier habitat in any other part of the world. From the Minoan art of Crete and Melos, it passed through the Mycenean, using the term to denote a later phase of Minoan art, to the art of the Geometric Age where it abounds on the pottery. Cretan pottery of the post-Mycenean Geometric style[4] shows no survival of the sign from the Geometric of the Minoan epoch. The only connecting link between these two Geometric styles is the Melian vase, Fig. 15, of an intermediate period.

The history of the pottery of Cyprus indirectly confirms the thesis that the swastika is peculiar to Minoan or Aegean civilization, for Cypri-

---

[1] Grammar of the Lotus, pp. 348ff.　　　　　[2] Compare above p. 119.

[3] G. Sergi, The Mediterranean Race, London, 1901.

[4] Annual of the British School at Athens, XII, J. B. Droop, Some Geometric Pottery from Crete, pp. 24ff.

ote art, which was a local developement quite distinct from Aegean, does not show the swastika in the Bronze Age when the great Minoan culture flourished. Even on Cypro-Mycenean fabrics the swastika is absent, doubtless because it is not at all frequent on Mycenean vases proper, though, as we have seen, local Mycenean ware at Melos, an island strongly under Minoan influence, shows the sign. On vases made in Cyprus during the early Iron Age, c. 1200-900 B. C., however, when the art was beginning to be subject to the influence of the new Geometric style, superseding the art of the Bronze Age and characteristic of most parts of Greece at this period, the swastika begins to appear. It is especially noteworthy to observe in what a tentative way the swastika gradually found a place on the scheme of ornamentation of Cypriote pottery. At first it is added to the vases of the indigenous Cypriote style as a plainly accessory device, quite isolated on the undecorated space of a vase. On nos. 502, 540 and 541 of Myres' catalogue of antiquities from the Cesnola collection in the Metropolitan Museum,[1] the swastika is to be seen just dropped as it were on the vase, not forming an integral part of the decoration. These pots belong to the early period of the Iron Age, c. 1200-900 B. C., when Cypro-Mycenean and pre-Mycenean survivals are found. There can be no doubt that the swastika at Cyprus is a pre-Mycenean survival.[2] Ohnefalsch-Richter many years ago traced the swastika in this island[3] to the Phoenicians who brought it by sea route from the East, while it arrived by overland route in Troy, or to Hissarlik. As we have seen, the theory of an eastern origin (i. e. India) is exploded, and if the sign were to be derived from Troy, it would have to be demonstrated at Cyprus in the very earliest part of the Bronze Age. The vase here illustrated, Plate XV, Fig. 18,[4] from the Cesnola collection showing the swastika as a mere accessory ornament belongs to Myres' Second Iron Age (the Middle or Geometric) period in Cyprus, c. 900-750 B. C.

The following, Plate XV, Figs. 19, 20,[5] are Greek Geometric vases found in Cyprus, but imported from Greece, also in the Cesnola collection. They are an oinochoë, Fig. 19, and a special form peculiar to the

[1] John L. Myres, Handbook of the Cesnola Collection of Antiquities from Cyprus, New York, 1914.

[2] The complete absence of the swastika on Bronze Age pottery in Cyprus, even on Cypro-Mycenean wares, indicates that it was through the medium of the Greek Geometric style that the sign was introduced into Cypriote Iron Age pottery.

[3] Bulletins de la Soc. d'Anthropologie de Paris, 1888, pp. 669ff.

[4] Myres, *op. cit.*, no. 598.　　　　　　　　　　　　[5] Ib. nos. 1702, 1701.

pottery of the Dipylon cemetery at Athens, Fig. 20. On each of these vases of the Geometric style belonging to the Iron Age (early part), are to be found numerous Bronze Age survivals, e. g. the double axe and swastika of Minoan art (in the panel of the oinochoë, above the horse, and, with rosette substituted for swastika, in the panels on the other vase); also, the motifs of the doe suckling her kid, and two deer confronting a sacred tree (in a single group in the panels repeated around the vase, Fig. 20). The frieze of tangent circles on both vases is reminiscent of Mycenean decoration. It is probable, therefore, that, through this indirect means of imported Greek Geometric pottery of the mainland, the swastika came from Minoan into Cypriote art.

The swastika continues to be found on Cypriote vases (of the Middle Geometric period in this island), always as a detached ornament (cf. Myres' catalogue *passim*). On the next illustration, Fig. 21,[1] the swastikas in the panel are worked into the decorative scheme in true Geometric style. This vase, formerly in the Cesnola collection, has been chosen to show what only a few of the monuments do, the unde-

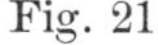

Fig. 21.   Fig. 22.

niable solar significance of the sign. For the symbol behind a goose or duck whose body takes the form of a solar disk with two triangular rays is enclosed within a solar halo. Another antiquity from Cyprus is the little four-horse chariot with driver and attendant, Fig. 22,[2] on which the wheel is ornamented by four swastikas between the spokes. The whole representation with the ray-like spokes suggests a solar interpretation. Both of these objects come from the Cesnola collection, and as they are not now in the Metropolitan Museum, we have not the

[1] Cesnola, Cyprus, App. p. 404, fig. 15.   [2] Cesnola, Salaminia, Fig. 226.

benefit of Myres' classification, and cannot assign them to a more definite date than between c. 900 and 750 B. C. Some terracotta figurines
from Cyprus (Wilson, Figs. 180, 181) of about this same period bear
the swastika on shoulders and arms, a clearly symbolic application of
the sign.

The next in order is a pinax or plate from Kameiros, Rhodes, Fig.
23,[1] which shows the swastika on that class of pottery known as Ionian,

Fig. 23.

a broad term including fabrics from Melos, Rhodes, Thera, Kyrene,
Daphnai and Naukratis, which were all about contemporaneous,
though probably somewhat later than the vases of the Geometric style.
Curiously enough the symbol occurs here also in connection with a
bird, goose or duck, as on the Cypriote vase, Fig. 21. On a space left
free on the wings of each of the two birds held by the neck by a
Gorgon, is a swastika. Another one is in the left field. Whether this
representation has a solar significance is a question not lightly to be
answered either way. Solar signs are often associated with birds (cf.
Déchelette's discussion of solar swans, Manuel, II, pp. 418ff.). It is
noteworthy at all events as another example besides the Cypriote vase,
Fig. 21, on which the sign appears with evident symbolic intent rather
than as a mere ornamental device as on many of the Geometric vases,
and on the following Rhodian vase, Fig. 24.[2] It will be noticed that

[1] London, British Museum. O. Keller, Thiere des class. Alterthums, 1887, p. 294, Fig. 51.
[2] K. F. Kinch, Vroulia (Rhodes), Berlin, 1914, Pl. 16, no. 2.

the sign has here the maeander-like form so often found on the Geometric pottery.

In concluding this section we give an example of a Boeotian clay model of a sarcophagus, or ossuary, the side, Fig. 25a, and the cover,

Fig. 24.

Fig. 25b.[1] While we cannot follow throughout Bertrand's speculative fancies in regard to the symbolic use of the swastika on Greek vases,[2] the scenes on this ossuary do not seem to be like the usual vase decorations, but to have a symbolic meaning. And then, too, we must remember that it was a funeral furnishing. The horse and a solar disk above, the figure of a winged deity or Gorgon with two birds in a hieratic pose, cf. Fig. 23, the so-called Persian Artemis Orientalizing type, and the serpents, and crosses and swastikas all seem to fit into a set of scenes appropriate to a funerary object.

As seen from the foregoing the swastika occurs on the Greek Geometric and Ionian wares in great abundance. Examples are figured in

---

[1] Boehlau, Böotische Vasen, Jahrbuch, 1888, p. 357 = Perrot et Chipiez, Histoire de l'Art dans l'Antiquité, X, Figs. 31, 32.

[2] *Op. cit.*, pp. 166ff. Note the swastikas on a vase painting of symbolic significance, Perrot et Chipiez, X, Fig. 30.

Wilson, from Melos, Thera, Naukratis, etc., and on proto-Attic and early Boeotian fabrics. Instances may also be found on proto-Corinthian ware,[1] but on later ceramic products it practically vanishes, until its

Fig. 25a.

Fig. 25b.

sudden revival on Attic red-figured vases of the Fine Style. For the prehistoric pottery we can assign only approximate limits. Déchelette (*op. cit.*) gives the following scheme for the chronology: Ist Iron Age, c. 1200-800 B. C., Period of the Dipylon or Geometric rectilinear decoration; IInd Iron Age, c. 800-480 B. C., Ionian and Archaic art. There is however no evidence from excavations on which we can base this exact classification of the Geometric and Ionian styles. All we know, in the present state of our knowledge, is that these two styles are subsequent to the Bronze Age Minoan and Mycenean pottery, and precede the early Attic, Boeotian and Corinthian styles. Whether any of the vases illustrated above goes back to quite as early a date as 1200 B. C. can not be definitely proved, though the period c. 1000-800 B. C. is a conservative dating. A transitional style must have intervened between the Minoan and Mycenean pottery of the Bronze Age,[2] and the Geometric pottery of the Iron Age, and yet that period could not have been very long, for the products are very scanty, so far as they are known at all, and the survival of Minoan motifs is an indication of a very close connection between the Geometric and preceding Minoan and Mycenean styles.

III. The Bronze and Iron Ages in Europe, c. 1200-500 B. C.

The symbol occurs on a great variety of prehistoric objects found in a wide belt extending across South Central Europe. As our first object has been to discover the original home-place of the sign, and this has been found in the Mediterranean basin, we need mention only

[1] Perrot et Chipiez, Histoire de l'Art, IX, p. 579, Fig. 292.
[2] Dragendorff, Thera, II, pp. 169ff.

a few examples from the continent of Europe. The hut urn, Fig. 26,[1] and the pottery fragments from the palafittes of Savoy, which have been claimed as perhaps the earliest known examples of the sign (cf. p. 119), have been here shown to belong to the latest period of the Bronze Age or beginning of the Iron Age, c. 1200-1000 B. C., and furthermore scarcely worthy to be cited as certain instances of the swas-

Fig. 26.

tika. There exist examples of the sign on bronze fibulae, however, which are of no uncertain character, and these fibulae are dated by Montelius in exactly the period under discussion. Fig. 27[2] shows the type of the fibula on which the swastika is found. Others are given in Montelius, *op. cit.*, I², Ser. B. Pl. 177. 3 and II², Ser. B. Pl. 257. 2. These fibulae come from Italy, and are common in the latter part of the Bronze Age, but rare in the Iron Age. They are the earliest objects from the South Central European region on which the swastika

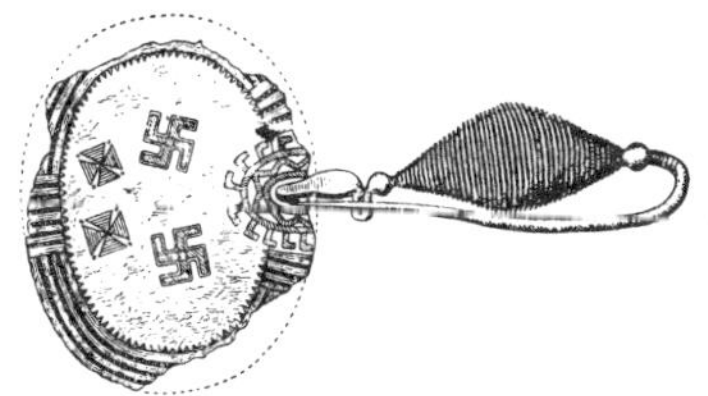

Fig. 27.

Fig. 28.

has thus far been known. In the Iron Age, the swastika is of frequent occurrence on bronze ornaments, repoussé belts, pottery, etc. Fig. 28[3] is a bronze ceinture from Hallstatt on which the swastika is worked

---

[1] Montelius, *op. cit.*, II¹, Ser. B. Pl. 140, 9b.   [2] Ibid. I¹, Ser. A. Pl. I. 9.
[3] De Mortillet, *op. cit.*, fig. 1255.

into the pattern as an ornamental device, but, in company with the cross with the four points which we have seen in Fig. 3 above, and which is surely of great antiquity. It may be seen on Bronze Age pottery from Cyprus.[1] A cross that is called the cross pommée is found here also in one of the upper diagonals. For this sign a great age can be established, for it is one of the hieroglyphic signs of Minoan script.[2] It suggests easily the well-known Ujjain symbol of Indian coins. On the ceinture it is accompanied by the four points as are also the swastika and the equal-armed or Greek cross.[3] In all these cases there may have been no symbolic value attached to the signs by maker or owner of this belt, but if this is so it is interesting then to note how a potent sign may at one time have a merely ornamental use without losing finally its symbolic significance. In fact, to prove a decorative use is not to annul the symbolic meaning. If the swastika is seen in ' vain repetitions ' on the flooring of a chemist's shop of to-day, as was the writer's experience recently, how does that differ from the occurrence of the sign on Roman mosaics?[4] And yet there is incontrovertible evidence for the symbolic use of the sign before and after the date of the mosaics. In the modern instance it is a survival lingering on, a vital

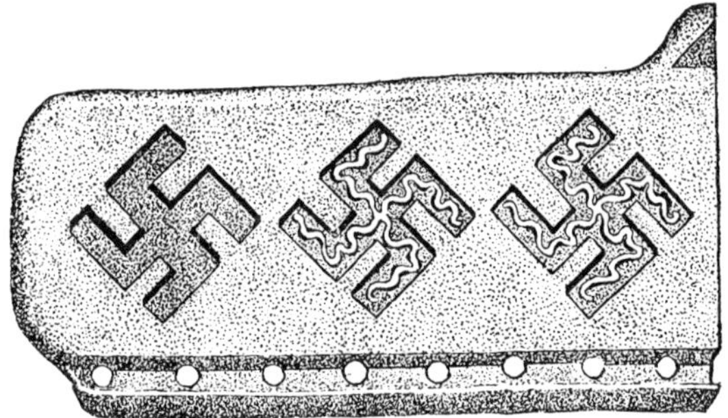

Fig. 29.

symbol that dies hard. In the Roman instance we have a parallel case to the use of the sign on the Greek Geometric vases where it also appears to be mere decoration. Another ceinture, Fig. 29,[5] comes from Koban in the Caucasus. In general, the swastika is rather common on objects coming from the cultural periods of Hallstatt, La Tène and Villanova. Déchelette (*op. cit.*) gives for these Iron Age cultures the

[1] J. L. Myres and M. Ohnefalsch-Richter. A Catalogue of the Cyprus Museum, Oxford, 1899, no. 400.

[2] Evans, Scripta Minoa, p. 222, no. 112.

[3] Compare a repoussé plaque from the forest of Hagenau, Bertrand, *op. cit.*, Pl. VII.

[4] Goblet d'Alviella, *op. cit.*, p. 35.

[5] E. Chantre, Nécropoles préhistoriques du Caucase, Pl. 11, 3.

following dates: Hallstatt, 900-700 B. C.; La Tène, 500-100 B. C. From South Central Europe the swastika spread over the entire continent as far north as Scandinavia, and as far west as Ireland. It is commonly acknowledged that the swastika is later in Northern and Western than in South Central Europe.

The swastikas on these Iron Age objects could be easily explained as derived from the Geometric pottery of Greece. The swastikas on the fibulae may not be accounted for in the same way, for some of these fibulae with the sign are assigned to the Bronze Age. In view of our inferential knowledge of communication by trade-routes overland and oversea between South Central Europe and Mediterranean centres (the types of weapons and decorative motives of the pottery of South Central European, late Neolithic and early Bronze [Copper] culture is closely paralleled with that of Cyprus, for example),[1] there is no difficulty in accounting for the presence of the swastika on South Central European Bronze objects. The ' migration ' may have been by the Bosphorus and Hellespont and through the Balkan peninsula. It would be unprofitable to attempt to trace the spread of the sign from one region to another in the prehistoric period with such a wide margin of speculation attached to every premise.

Fig. 30.

IV. The Historical Period in Greece, c. 600-200 B. C.

The history of the swastika in Greece after its widespread use on vases of the prehistoric period is rather curious. In Cyprus it disap-

[1] Myres and O-Richter, *op. cit.*, p. 19.

pears after the Fifth Century B. C. It is rarely found on Greek pottery after the Ionian fabrics, though occasional examples are cited with the sign as a part of a garment design.[1] On coins we have it rather early, as for instance on the uncertain Ionian electrum, Pl. XVI, 1. We shall treat the coins separately from the other objects, and turn our attention to three examples of the sign on vases dating about 400-200 B. C., which are of very unusual interest as showing the swastika as a symbolic sign in an even more unmistakable manner than any of the preceding examples except Figs. 2, 11, 21, 23. The first is of crowning importance for the meaning of the sign. It is a red-figured vase painting, Fig. 30,[2] from a krater of Apulian provenance, in the Kunsthistorisches Museum in Vienna,[3] representing Apollo in a quadriga surrounded by a radiate disk, bearing on his breast a swastika. This decoration of the chiton of Apollo, like the other motives, marks his exclusive character as a sun-god, and we may therefore call him Helios. It is a picture of the rising sun, the radiate belt and rayed ornamentation around the neck of the chiton, the sun-disks (plain circles) on the belt and to right and left of the swastika are all solar ornaments like the central device, the

Fig. 31.Fig. 32.

swastika. The other two figures from vases Figs. 31,[4] 32,[5] show the swastika with evident symbolic intent, the one on the short chiton of a warrior, above and below the belt, possibly, as has been suggested, as

[1] Bertrand, *op. cit.*, Fig. 27.

[2] T. Panofka, Archaeolog. Zeitung, 1848, pl. 20. 1. Our figure is taken from A. B. Cook's Zeus, Fig. 269. Compare Bertrand, *op. cit.*, p. 171, n. 1, on the established authenticity of the swastika on this vase.

[3] E. von Sacken und Fr. Kenner, Die Samml. des K. K. Münz- und Antiken-Cabinetes, Vienna, 1866, p. 241 (no. 259). This vase is one of the Lower Italian fabrics, judging from its find-place, style and the collection to which it belongs.

[4] Paris, Louvre K, 405, Bertrand, *op. cit.*, Pl. XIX. 1.

[5] Daremberg et Saglio, Dict. des Antiq., art. *Cingulum*, p. 1177.

a prophylakterion or protective symbol placed over the vital parts. The belt of this warrior is also ornamented with a solar wheel, which may have a prophylactic meaning, as we believe we shall be able to show in the course of this study of symbols. On the other vase the swastika is placed on the ' apron ' of the warrior, charging with spear in hand as in the former case, and its prophylactic meaning can not be doubted. The presence of a solar device, solar wheel on the horse's haunch, like that on the belt of the first warrior, brings these two vase-figures very close in regard to the significance of their symbols.

V. The Roman and Gallo-Roman Epochs.

Aside from coins (cf. Pl. XVI. 20), no monuments of the Roman period have been cited except mosaics in which the swastika appears as a decorative motif (Goblet d'Alviella, *op. cit.*, p. 35).[1] In the Gallo-

Fig. 33.   Fig. 34.

Roman epoch the swastika is met with on altars, Figs. 33,[2] 34.[3] One of these, Fig. 33, has a wheel as central ornament. L. Müller figures another altar with a swastika flanked by two wheels, dedicated to Jupiter Optimus Maximus (I. O. M.).[4] Since the wheel among the Gauls was a solar emblem[5] (as among the Greeks), it is possible that the swastika and wheels on this altar are signs related to the national solar deity of the Gauls, here assimilated to the Roman Jupiter. The anony-

---

[1] See also the swastika-like mosaic in the orchestra (Roman period) of the theatre at Athens, Cook, *op. cit.*, Pl. XXIX.

[2] Bertrand, *op. cit.*, Fig. 7.

[3] Ibid., Fig. 9.   De Mortillet, *op. cit.*, Fig. 1267 = Wilson, Fig. 220, Musée de Toulouse.

[4] *Op. cit.*, Fig. 29.   Goblet d'Alviella, *op. cit.*, p. 50.

[5] H. Gaidoz, Le Dieu Gaulois du Soleil et le Symbolisme de la Roue, Paris, 1886.

mous altars, Figs. 33 and 34, may then relate to a solar god, for, being uninscribed th... ppi are apparently not tombstones.[1]

...n-Christian Period.

Perhaps the most interesting examples of the swastika are those occurring on funerary inscriptions and in paintings in the catacombs.

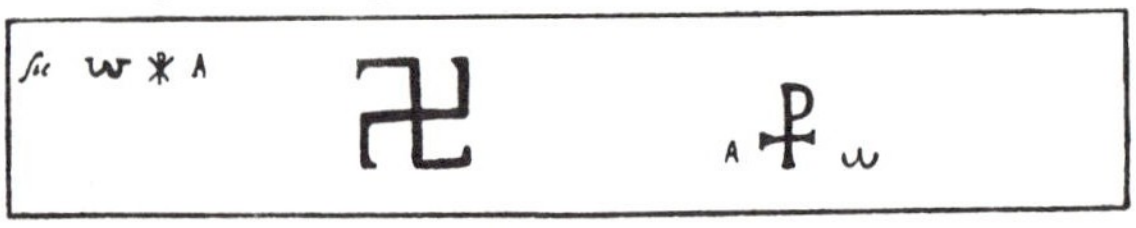

Fig. 35.

The fact that the Christians adopted this pagan symbol shows how vital a symbol it must have been in pagan superstition. The following, Figs. 35,[2] and 36,[3] are taken from Bertrand's Pl. IX on which several

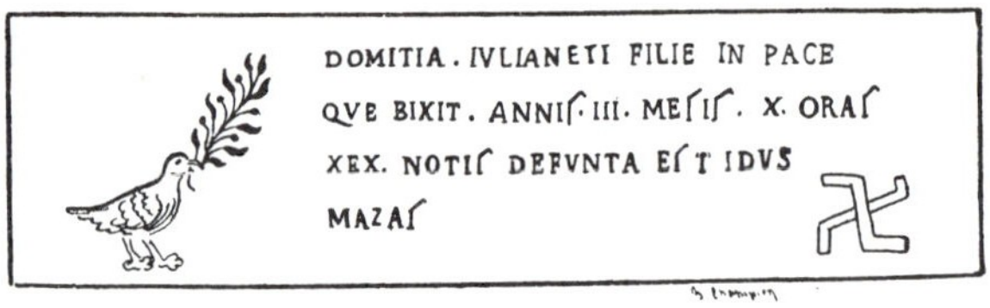

Fig. 36.

instances are given. The statement is often made that the Christians employed the swastika 'cross' to conceal their own Christian cross. This argument however will not 'hold water' in view of such inscriptions as Figs. 35 and 36, on which the Chrism or Christ-monogram and other conspicuous Christian symbols appear with the swastika, an open display of the faith of the defunct. The swastika among the Christians is a survival, a mystic sign borrowed because of its potency as a magic sign or talisman. Whatever meaning it had for them, its magic value as the Christians felt it, is the impression that we derive to-day from observing its use on their monuments. From the three noteworthy catacomb paintings cited by Bertrand showing the swastika on the garments of real and mythological figures, we have selected that of the grave-digger, Diogenes Fossor, from the Coemeterium of Petrus and Marcellinus, Fig. 37.[4] The sign seems to have the generalized meaning of something protective or apotropaic. The lower register (cf. Bertrand, *op. cit.*, Pl. IX) contains a representation of Christ, so that the theory of the swastika being a dissimulated Christian cross has no support whatever from this painting, as we saw was the case with

[1] Other examples cited by Bertrand, p. 145, n. 5, now in the Musée de St. Germain-en-Laye.
[2] Bertrand, *op. cit.*, Pl. IX. [3] Ibid., Pl. IX.
[4] Ibid., Pl. X, upper register only.

the inscriptions. To the Christian period belong also the swastikas embroidered on mummy-cloth from Egypt,[1] and carved on tombstones in Asia Minor.[2] Christian lamps show the sign not infrequently.[3] The

Fig. 37.

catacomb swastikas are dated at the earliest towards the end of the Third Century.

VII.   The Swastika in India and China.

It is a difficult matter to date the earliest use of the sign in India, for no material has been published from which to gather reliable data. On the coins, we shall not find the symbol before the Fourth Century B. C. at the earliest. Examples on other Indian monuments may exist prior to this date, but we have no data on this subject from researches on the swastika in Indian art. The fact that the grammarian Pāṇini who is said to have lived about 350 B. C., incorporated in his work the word used by the Indians for the sign, taken in conjunction with the numismatic evidence, gives ground for postulating the use of the symbol in the Fourth and perhaps the Fifth Centuries B. C. It may also be concluded that it was brought to India from Greece. It has been established above that its earliest use was in the Mediterranean lands,

---

[1] Wilson, *op. cit.*, Fig. 136.

[2] A. Margaret Ramsay, Isaurian and East-Phrygian Art in the Third and Fourth Centuries after Christ (Studies in the History and Art of the Eastern Provinces of the Roman Empire, ed. by W. M. Ramsay, Aberdeen, 1906), Figs. 12, 14, 16, 19, 20, 27. These instances on Christian gravestones from the eastern part of the Empire, belong to the Third and Fourth Centuries, and show how deep a hold the swastika symbol had upon all Christian communities.

[3] Kaufmann (cf. Introd. p. 90), p. 603.

and, just preceding the time when it seems first to appear in India, there was considerable commercial contact between these two countries. "During the Persian rule from the time of Darius, circ. B. C. 500, down to Alexander's conquest B. C. 327, there was constant intercourse between India and the West," writes Head in the Historia Numorum,[2] p. 832, in his introductory sentence on the coinage of Bactria and North-west India. It was not however through the medium of coins that the swastika was introduced into India, for as we shall see, its use on Greek coins is extremely restricted, and, furthermore, it does not occur at all on the coins issued by the Greek successors of Alexander in India, the Greco-Bactrian series. As indicated above, its appearance in India is evidently earlier than the Greco-Bactrian coins. It must therefore have been through the pottery that the sign was carried to India. Fig. 41[1] is one of the monuments most often cited for the

Fig. 41.

swastika in India, the so-called footprints of Buddha from the Amaravati tope. Here the swastika is seen in conjunction with various symbols, some solar. We shall not go into the details of the swastika in the East, as it was not indigenous there but borrowed. In China, Japan and Tibet no monuments have been cited which would conflict with a theory of derivation from India through the medium of the Buddhists. The symbol was, and is still, according to abundant testimony, used by Buddhists and Brahmins in India, and it was doubtless carried by them into China and Japan. A notable fact is the evidence given by Wilson (*op. cit.*, pp. 800ff.) that the swastika enclosed in a

[1] Wilson, *op. cit.*, Fig. 32.

circle was a new form of character introduced into Chinese writing by the Empress Wu (c. 704-684 B. C.) of the Tang Dynasty, as a sign for 'sun.' The meaning of the sign in India, at least its modern use, is that of 'benediction, luck, blessing.' This sense would not conflict with an original use in the meaning of 'sun' or the sun's course in the heavens, whatever the sign stood for to the Greeks, for the latter-day sense of many a symbol is often purely general. In fact on the examples from America, the sign seems to have some solar connotation, and yet the oral testimony of people who have lived among those Indians who use the sign is to the effect that the meaning which they give to it is that of 'luck.' (Wilson, *op. cit.*, p. 895.)

VIII.   The Swastika in America.

Wilson gives a number of examples of varying value to prove the existence of the sign in America. Those which are undoubted instances are from the North American Indians, the Kansas, Sacs and Navajos. The sign embroidered on bead-work composed of ancient motifs (*op. cit.*, Pl. 15), and the sandpoint drawing (ib. Pl. 17), establish its present-day use, and its probable prehistoric (i. e. before 1500 A. D.) usage in America. Pottery from Central Mexico in the Natural History Museum of New York shows the sign as an ornamental motif.[1] An example from Peru is cited on a stone vase.[2] The shell gorgets shown in Wilson seem rather dubious cases. More important than any of the evidence from monuments is the testimony gathered among the tribes which goes to show that the sign is still, in America as in the East, regarded as a magic or good-luck symbol.

IX.   The Swastika as a Mystic or Cabalistic Sign.

Under this caption we may include instances of the swastika where there is no trace of a religious or sacred use of the sign, and where it appears to be employed without any regard to any especial or traditional meaning, where from association it may be regarded as cabalistic. This is the case with some Danish bracteates, Fig 42, a - c, dating from the Fifth to the Ninth Century A. D.[3] These gold medallic ornaments were worn as charms and bear frequently (a, b) meaningless inscrip-

---

[1] Two bowls, with orange and red decoration, of the Toltec period.

[2] T. A. Joyce, South American Archaeology, New York, 1912, p. 207, Fig. 26, fragment of a stone cup from Tiahuanaco, Bolivia, in the British Museum.

[3] Kongl. Vitterhets, etc., Manadsblad, 1873, p. 3, Fig. 3; p. 379, Fig. 5; Forvännen, 1906, p. 135, Fig. 3.   Cf. L. Müller, *op. cit.*, and R. Forrer, Reallexikon, Taf. 136. 3, 5–7.

tions in Runic letters. On (b) and (c) the symbol is plain, while on (a) the form is similar to examples from China shown in Wilson (*op. cit.*, Fig. 31), and in Bertrand (*op. cit.*, Pl. VI). In view of the analogy, the sign on this bracteate as well, may be regarded as a swastika,

a.   b.   c.

Fig. 42.

with the ends prolonged by another right-angled turn or arm. It may be thought that the Christian use of the swastika, and the use of the sign in general as a prophylactic or talismanic emblem is of the same character as that of the present examples. But we have to exclude all other cases as possibly containing some significance, the essence of which we cannot of course with certainty discern. The Christians in all probability used the sign as a cross symbol, not to conceal their faith, as sometimes stated, but simply as another cross symbol, which they may have regarded as a pagan forerunner of their own cross.[1] Mystic, doubtless the usage of the sign often was, but its presence on these charms warrants a separate classification of these amulets, as examples of a different phase of the symbol, namely, its use as a purely cabalistic emblem.

X. The Swastika on Coins.

I. *Greece. Sixth to Fourth Century B. C., and later.*

Uncertain of Ionia

1. Obv. Swastika turning to right, enclosed in a square.
El hemi-hekte or twelfth. 1.16 gr. London. Pl. XVI. 1.

B. M. C. Ionia, Pl. I. 13. Babelon, Traité II¹, no. 99, Pl. III. 24 (no. 100, same type, ¹⁄₉₆ of a stater).

This coin belongs to the Uncertain class of early electrum assigned by Babelon to Southern Ionia. The conjectural attribution to Corinth

---

[1] This opinion is confirmed by the Isaurian tombstones of Christians referred to in Section VI, on which the prominent swastika is the only ' cross ' symbol. In these cases, the swastika was certainly a substitute for the Christian cross.

in the B. M. C. is due to the swastika-like incuse of the Corinthian coins of the first period, at one time the most familiar swastika on Greek coins.

Fig. 43.

2. Obv. Curvilinear swastika, turning to left, with four points in the angles of intersection of the arms; enclosed in a square (?) within zigzag lines, or star pattern. El hekte. 2.92 gr. London. Fig. 43.

B. M. C. Ionia, Pl. II. 20 = Traité II¹, Pl. IX. 18 (also hemi-hekte, 1.38 gr. Boston. Regling, Samml. Warren, Pl. XXXVII. 1709).

This figure with central boss at the intersection of the curving lines might pass for a tetraskeles as well as a swastika which we have called it. But the swastika on Indian coins is sometimes very close in form to the present example, even to the central boss; and the four points we have already seen in connection with the sign at an early date (cf. pp. 117, 128). Again, the original Lycian symbol, at least on coins, is a three-armed figure, and has the arms, three (and later, four) centering about a circle, which only on later coins becomes reduced to a central boss or dot. This figure may well be counted as a true swastika. Coins 1 and 2 belong to the Sixth or Seventh Century B. C.

Akanthos, Macedonia

3. Obv. Forepart of a bull, kneeling l. with head reverted; above, a swastika, turning to r.
Æ triobol. 2.27 gr. Paris. Pl. XVI. 2.
Traité II¹, Pl. LIV. 17. Cf. B. M. C. Macedonia, nos. 33, 34.

4. Similar, with Γ and swastika.
Æ triobol. 2.54 gr. Pl. XVI. 3.
Catalogue Rhousopoulos, Hirsch XIII, Pl. XI. 801.

These coins belong to the Fifth Century, c. 500-424 B. C.

Astakos, Bithynia

5. Rev. Head of a nymph; behind, a swastika, turning to r.
Æ drachm. 4.90 gr. Milan. Pl. XVI. 4.
Traité II², Pl. CLXXXI. 1 (cf. triobol, *op. cit.*, Pl. CLXXXI. 2).

The head on these coins is of archaic style, and the date is not later than c. 480 B. C.

Thaliadai, Arcadia

6. Rev. Swastika, turning to l. in shallow incuse square.
Æ obol. 1.01 gr. Berlin. Pl. XVI. 5.

Traité II¹, Pl. XXXVIII. 22.

The obverse type of this coin, Hermes running, permits us to assign it to a date not later than the coin of Astakos above.

Fig. 44 (enlarged two diameters).

Mesembria, Thrace

7.   Rev. Rayed wheel, with the three first letters of the ethnic, MEϟ, followed by a swastika, inscribed between the four spokes.

Æ obol.   0.31 gr.   London.   Pl. XVI. 6, and Fig. 44.

B. M. C. Thrace, no. 4.   Gardner, Numismatic Chronicle, 1880, p. 60.

This little coin of Mesembria, very rare if not unique, has already been mentioned as of paramount importance for the interpretation of the swastika.   Its date is c. 400-300 B. C.

Thasos, Thrace

8.   Rev. Herakles kneeling r. shooting; in r. field, swastika, turning to r.

Æ tetradrachm.   15.29 gr.   Jameson.   Pl. XVI. 7.

Coll. R. Jameson, Pl. LV. 1070 (ex. Cat. Rhousopoulos, Hirsch XIII, Pl. XI. 681).

The coins of this type with the swastika symbol are rare.   They date c. 411-400 B. C.

Kromna, Paphlagonia

9.   Rev. Head of nymph or of Hera with turreted stephanos, above which, a swastika turning to l.

Æ drachm.   3.50 gr.   Paris.   Pl. XVI. 8.

Traité II², Pl. CLXXXIV. 1.   Another specimen is in the Jameson collection with swastika turning to r., Coll. R. Jameson, Pl. LXX. 1369.

The date of this coin is c. 340-300 B. C.   Jameson, *op. cit.*, places his example 'towards 300 B. C.'

Philip II, Macedonia

10.   Rev. Horseman r.; beneath, monogram and swastika, turning to r.

Æ tetrobol, 2.50 gr.   Glasgow.   Pl. XVI. 9.

Macdonald, Cat. of Hunterian Coll. I, p. 293, no. 106.

This rare coin was issued after c. 336 B. C.[1]

Damastion, Illyricum

11.   Rev. Tripod-lebes; between the legs, two swastikas, turning to l.

Æ stater, 12.70 gr.   London.   Pl. XVI. 10.

B. M. C. Thessaly, Pl. XV. 12.

[1] This is the opinion of Mr. Newell who has not yet published the results of his researches on this group of the Macedonian regal issues.

12.   Rev. Square ingot with strap for carrying, on which is a swastika, turning to r.

Æ drachm, 3.11 gr.   London.   Pl. XVI. 11.

B. M. C. Thessaly, Pl. XVI. 5.   Cf. Imhoof-Blumer, Monn. gr. p. 135, and Beiträge zur Münzkunde in the Zeitschrift für Numismatik, 1874, p. 111, and Pl. III.

13.   Rev. Miner's pick-axe and swastika, turning to r.

Fig. 45.

Æ hemi-drachm, 1.63 gr.   Fig. 45.

Imhoof-Blumer, ib. Pl. III. 18.

These coins are Fourth-Century issues of the Illyrio-Epirote city, Damastion.   The reverse types of nos. 12 and 13, the cast metal ingot and the miner's pick, bear witness to the mining industry of this town whose silver mines are mentioned by Strabo, VII, p. 326.

Rhegion, Bruttium

14.   Rev. Head of Apollo r. ; under chin, swastika, turning to r.

Æ tetradrachm, 17.41 gr.   (Formerly Fenerly Bey).   Pl. XVI. 12.

Cat. Fenerly Bey, Egger XLI, Pl. III. 86.

This very rare tetradrachm which is lacking in the B. M. catalogue and Garrucci, was mentioned by Müller, Det Saakaldte Hagekors, and illustrated on his p. 16, Fig. 17.   His reference was a communication from Imhoof-Blumer who had referred to it in the Z. f. Num., 1874, p. 113, and the coin there noted is perhaps now in the Berlin collection. The present example is probably not the identical coin cited by Imhoof ; it is not unedited, at any rate, even though it may be unique.   Its date is c. 415-387 B. C.

Panormos, Sicily

15.   Rev. Head of a nymph to r., hair worn in long roll on neck ; behind, swastika, turning to l.   (Obv. Hound standing l.)

Æ didrachm, 8.56 gr.   Jameson.   Pl. XVI. 13.

Coll. R. Jameson, Pl. XXXII. 686.

16.   Rev. Head of a nymph to r., with hair in a sphendone ; behind, a swastika, turning to r. ; inscription ΓΑΝΟΡΜΙΤΙΚΟΝ   (Obv. Hound standing r., with head reverted ; above, murex shell.)

a)   Æ didrachm, 8.49 gr.   London.   Pl. XVI. 14.

B. M. C., Sicily, p. 121, no. 2.   Hill, Coins of Ancient Sicily, p. 93, Fig. 18.

b) Æ didrachm, 7.84 gr.   Jameson.

Cat. Jameson Coll., Pl. XXXIII, 692.

Of these two coin types, no. 15 is much earlier than no. 16. It is anepigraphic, and the hound on the obverse stands towards the left. On account of the general similarity of the types of no. 15 to the Panormite types of no. 16 and the presence of the swastika on it, the coin no. 15 has been assigned by Jameson to Panormos. It is very rare, and if ascribed to Panormos, would be one of the earliest known issues of that mint. For, the style is not more advanced than on the tetradrachms of Syracuse of the period, c. 479-466 B. C. (Head's Syracuse, Pl. II). The more common coins with the ethnic of the type of no. 16 show no such traces of archaism as are seen in this head of still strong Transitional style. A head on a Syracusan tetradrachm very similar in technical achievement and arrangement of the hair is one in Jameson's catalogue, Pl. XXXVII. 764, 'vers 470' according to the author. It seems more probable that this coin should belong to Panormos than to Segesta which had the hound and nymph types, for the latter coinage bears regularly the ethnic, and commences at a period earlier than the present uninscribed coin. Motya and Eryx had also these coin types, but in these cases, as at Panormos, the types were probably original with Segesta. The coin no. 16 may be dated between 450 and 420 B. C.

Uncertain of Sicily, ZIZ Series

17.   Obv. Head of a nymph r. wearing a sphendone ; behind, a swastika, turning to l.   (Rev. Forepart of a man-headed bull r.)

Æ litra or obol, 0.62 gr.   London.

B. M. C. Sicily, p. 249, no. 22.   Hill, Sicily, p. 246, note 1.

18.   Obv. Young male head l. ; behind, swastika, turning to l.   (Rev. Man-headed bull standing l. ; above, Punic inscription *sch baal*.)

Æ litra, 0.62 gr.   Jameson.   Pl. XVI. 15.

Coll. R. Jameson, Pl. XXXIV. 695.   Holm, Geschichte Siciliens, III, Pl. VIII. 18.   B. M. C. Sicily, p. 249, no. 29.

19.   Rev. Head of Persephone l. surrounded by dolphins ; under her chin, a swastika, turning to r.   (Rev. Quadriga, and Punic inscription *Ziz*.)

a) Æ tetradrachm, 16.78 gr.   Jameson (formerly Evans).   Pl. XVI. 16.

Coll. R. Jameson, Pl. XXXIV. 69.   A. J. Evans, Num. Chron. 1891, Pl. XV. 4.

b) Similar with swastika *behind* the head, turning to *l*.

Æ tetradrachm, 16.77 gr.   London.

B. M. C. Sicily, p. 248, no. 13.

The variety described under (a) is perhaps unique, while (b) has probably not been illustrated. The types are copied from the Syracusan medallion of Euainetos.

20. Obv. Female head l. with diadem, on front of which is a swastika. (Rev. Quadriga and *Ziz.*)

Evans, Num. Chron. 1891, p. 370, no. 61.   Imhoof-Blumer, Zeit. f. Num. 1874, p. 113.

Of this type five (or six) examples were discovered in a hoard of coins found in Western Sicily (Evans, *op. cit.* and A. Salinas, Notizie degli Scavi, 1888). Imhoof-Blumer also mentioned the type which seems not to have been illustrated so far. It is a tetradrachm of the Phoenician class imitated from a Kimon type of Syracuse like the one shown in B. M. C. Sicily, p. 247, no. 8, but having the swastika on the ampyx (cf. Addenda, p. 154, Fig. 49).

The coins bearing the Punic letters *Ziz*, an unexplained word, are for convenience usually grouped under Panormos. Scholars are by no means agreed however that *Ziz* is 'simply the Phoenician name for Panormos' as Head (H. N.² p. 162) wrote (cf. Macdonald, Hunter. Coll. I, p. 207, note, and Imhoof-Blumer, Num. Zeitschrift, 1886, pp. 263ff). The objections to this interpretation are numerous. Holm (*op. cit.*, p. 670) has discussed the question the most recently, and agrees with Imhoof that Panormos cannot be held to be the mint of the great variety of coins (with types reminiscent of Motya, Eryx, Syracuse, Segesta, etc.) which bear the *Ziz* inscription. He writes, " In the whole coinage, the types betray the obvious striving to adapt themselves to all possible cities of Sicily, naturally with the cities of the West taking precedence, as of course is consistent with the Phoenician inscription. Thus, as far as the types go, there is no indication which points to a single city as the mint-place." However, there exists, he continues, the coin with *Ziz* on one side, and ΓΑΝΟΡΜΟΣ on the other. From this may be concluded, that *Ziz* refers to Panormos, whether as the Punic equivalent for the name of the city or as an appellation of the same cannot be determined. But, Holm's argument shows, this is not saying that *Ziz* always means Panormos, though it is reasonable to infer that it does on the coin here instanced (Macdonald, Hunter. Coll. I, Pl. XV. 10). Holm's solution of the paradox of *Ziz* standing for Panormos on some coins and not for it on others, is, then, the following : *Ziz* designates a series of issues struck by the Carthaginians and their allies in Sicily, probably begun before the great invasion of 409 B. C. Panormos as a prominent Phoenician town·was one of the first to strike these coins with *Ziz*, and other cities soon followed suit, to wit, Motya and Eryx. This was the first group of *Ziz* coins. Later, a more widespread series was minted, Bundesmünzen, Holm calls them, since they were, he thinks, alliance issues of the non-Greek and hostile population. These comprise (a) tetradrachms imitated from Syracusan medallions of Kimon and Euainetos, and (b) smaller denominations of different local types for local use. The word *Ziz* therefore though originally meaning Panormos, came to signify in effect ' issue of the Carthaginians in Sicily.' Holm's theory is a plausible solution of the *Ziz* puzzle, and Imhoof has shown that certain *Ziz* coins of Motyan types are connected by identical dies (Num. Zeit. 1886, Pl. VII. 1-4) with coins actually bearing the ethnic, and that the *Ziz* coins of Motyan types were therefore struck in the same mint as the regular series.

Eryx, Sicily

21. Rev. Hound standing r. ; above, swastika, turning to r. (Obv. Nymph seated, playing with dove.)

Æ litra, 0.92 gr. London. Pl. XVI. 17.

B. M. C. Sicily, p. 62, no. 10. Hill, Sicily, Pl. IX. 10. Another example is in the Jameson collection, 0.74 gr., Pl. XXVIII. 571.

This type is dated by Head and Hill c. 413-400 B. C.

Motya, Sicily

22. Rev. Head of a nymph r., hair bound four times with a cord : surrounded by three dolphins, below ⊟. (Obv. Horseman with MOTVAION.)

a) Æ didrachm, 7.80 gr. Glasgow.

Macdonald, *op. cit.*, I, p. 205.

b) 8.60 gr. (cited by Imhoof-Blumer, Zur Münzkunde Grossgriechenlands, Num. Zeit. XVIII, 1886, p. 253, Pl. VII. 1). Pl. XVI. 18.

c) 8.60 gr. Jameson.

Coll. R. Jameson, Pl. XXXII. 665.

23. Same reverse type and die as no. 22, combined with hound and nymph's head type as on Segestan coins.

Imhoof-Blumer, *op cit.*, Pl. VII. 2.

These coins of Motya with Greek inscription (no. 22, a-c) were struck within the period 480-420 B. C. Jameson assigns his example (c) which is of identical head though not the same die as (a and b) to the date c. 430 B. C., an appropriate date for the style. The symbol under the chin of the nymph's head seems to be a badly formed swastika.

The earliest occurrence of the swastika in Sicily is on coins of towns distinctly Phoenician or under Phoenician influence, Panormos, Eryx and the *Ziz* coinage of Panormos, etc., issued by the Phoenicians in Sicily. It might, therefore, be expected also at Motya, and these coins show that it perhaps did occur there, though the sign has not before been recognized as such. (Macdonald, *op. cit.*, calls the sign a ' swastika-like figure ').

Since the swastika was not originally a Phoenician symbol we must infer that the Phoenicians found it still in use in Western Sicily, at the time of their intrusion, and we do not need to assume a special survival of Minoan tradition to account for this.[1] For, the wide-spread occurrence of the symbol in Greek lands, at points scattered all the way from Ionia to Sicily, without trace of inter-dependence, can only be explained as survivals of a general usage, a conclusion entirely in harmony with the other archaeological evidence.

Syracuse, Sicily

24. Rev. Swastika, turning to l.

Æ 20mm. Newell. Pl. XVI. 19.

Another specimen in the Cat. Rhousopoulos, Pl. VI. 454, shows narrower arms. This type whose obverse bears a head of Zeus Eleutherios would naturally belong to the time of the Democracy, 345-317 B. C. (so Head, H. N². p. 180). This necessitates or implies the placing of the coin with similar obverse, but reverse with triskeles (B. M. C. Sicily, no. 354, given to time of Agathokles, 317-289 B. C.) among the issues of the Democracy (cf. Macdonald, Hunter. Cat. I, p. 238, note). The triskeles was not then original with Agathokles, but appropriated by him from an earlier coin type. As we shall see, the triskeles of three human legs, which may be called the Sicilian symbol to distinguish it from the three-armed symbol known as the Lycian symbol, was used on Greek coinage at a period antedating the use of the Lycian symbol on coins. Agathokles doubtless was the first to use it as a personal badge,[2] and it probably became later the sign for the three-pointed island, the ' Trinakria ' of the Greeks.

Latium with Campania. Central Italian Communities, Uncertain Mint

25. Rev. Swastika, turning to l.

Æ 29mm. Pl. XVI. 20.

Hirsch Cat. XXXIV, Pl. XXIV. 622 = Haeberlin, Aes Grave, Pl. 68. 26, and Garrucci, Monete dell'Italia Antica, Pl. XLII. 5. (Haeberlin, ib. Pl. 68. 27, same type to l.).

[1] Evans, Annual of the British School at Athens, IX, 1902–3, p. 60.

[2] Hill, Sicily, p. 152, suggests that it may have been the private signet of Agathokles.

This last example of the swastika occurs on an uncia of the Aes Grave of Central Italy dated by Haeberlin 'after 334 B. C.' It is possible chronologically that the type was here copied from the preceding type of Syracuse, and, as the symbol is formed in the same way, the borrowing becomes quite probable. At Syracuse the sign was very likely first suggested by the Phoenician coinage, especially the tetradrachm issues imitating Syracusan medallions.

Fig. 46.

Thaena, Byzacene, North Africa

26. Rev. Bust of Astarte, to left of which swastika turning to r., with Punic inscription, *Thainath.*

Æ 28mm. Fig. 46.

Müller, Numismatique de l'Ancienne Afrique, p. 40, no. 4.

The obverse of this type bears the head of Augustus. The occurrence of the swastika at this late date is somewhat remarkable. Its presence on the coinage of this Phoenician town is not strange now that we have seen that the sign in Sicily is due to Phoenician influence. But it does seem odd that we have no connecting link between the Punic issues in Sicily of no later date than the Fourth Century (early part), and this coin of Roman times.

Fig. 47.

Gaul, Senones (?)

27. Obv. Young, beardless head, laureate r.; behind, swastika, turning to r. (Rev. Eagle on thunderbolt with inscription GIAMILOS.)

Æ 17mm. Fig. 47.

Müller, *op. cit.,* p. 21, Fig. 27. Duchalais, Déscr. des Médailles Gauloises de la Bibliothèque Royale, no. 617. Blanchet, Traité des Monnaies Gauloises, p. 361, Fig. 322 (similar type without the swastika).

The head on this bronze coin of Northeastern Gaul is imitated from the denarii of the Roman Republic belonging to the First Century B.C.

28.   Obv. Head l. with hair in S-shaped locks, forming a swastika figure.
N 21mm.   3.35–4.02 gr.   Fig. 48a, b.
Blanchet, Traité, p. 323, Figs. 233, 234.   Müller, *op. cit.*, p. 20, Fig. 26.

a.   b.
Fig. 48.

This type is one of the rich series of gold staters issued in North western Gaul.   The curious device may be accepted as a swastika with reserve, for it is not an undoubted case like that on no. 27.   Swastika combinations occur, however, on coins of the Aduatuci (Bertrand, *op. cit.*, Fig. 13, Blanchet, Traité, Fig. 317) and elsewhere (cf. Blanchet, ib., Index).   The simple form, not rectilinear, but curvilinear, occurs as type on coins found in Gaul, perhaps belonging to the northern part, Blanchet, Traité, Figs. 21, 22.

In concluding the section on Greek coins, it should be remarked that the statement of Goblet d'Alviella (*op. cit.* p. 40), quoted after him by Wilson (*op. cit.* p. 807) to the effect that the swastika is found on coins of the Arsacidae and Sassanidae is erroneous.   The same should be said of various and sundry implications that the swastika occurs ' frequently ' or ' exclusively ' on coins with the head of Apollo or with Apolline insignia or with Zeus, etc.   From the foregoing it will be perfectly clear that the symbol has no special connection with the type, except on the Mesembrian coin.   The reverses, Pl. XVI. 22-26, having a swastika-like design are : Pantikapaion, 22, Corinth, 23, 24, Eïon, 25, and Apollonia Pontica, 26.   No. 21 is here shown as a case which should not be confused with the swastika reverse, for it is not a reverse type, but an obverse having as design a raised or negative incuse design, having no connection with the swastika.   The other reverses (and several others on Greek coins) may with great probability be considered as influenced by the swastika pattern.

Fig. 48ᴬ.

Fig. 48ᴬ shows another example of the swastika reverse.   This is one of the coins of the Trésor d'Auriol group (with a ram's head on the obverse), which show reverses akin to this incuse design.   The resemblance to the swastika is not so marked on all of the reverses of this type, but yet it does not seem to be purely accidental, since incuses in general do not naturally suggest the swastika design.   This figure and the following, Fig. 49, are reproduced after photographs from the original coins.

Fig. 49.

ADDENDA

Page 149, no. 20.   A coin of the type here noted is the following, Fig. 49, Æ tetradrachm, 16.85 gr., in the collection of Mr. Newell, showing very distinctly the swastika (to r.) on the ampyx.

II.   India.   Fourth Century B. C. to Tenth Century A. D. (and perhaps later)

The earliest example known to us is the coin, Pl. XVI. <u>27</u>, a rectangular punch-marked copper coin, dating c. 300 or 400 B. C. (V. A. Smith, Cat. of the Coins in the Indian Museum, Calcutta, Pl. XIX. 10). It was struck possibly at Taxila in the Panjab (*op. cit.*, p. 133).   It bears a curvilinear swastika in a circula incuse as a punch-mark.   No. 28 (with elephant as obverse) is a rectangular double-die coin of Taxila of a type issued from about 350 B. C. (cf. Cunningham, Coins of Ancient India, Pl. III. 1, and Smith, *op. cit.*, Pl. XX. 9).   No. 29 is a single-die coin also of Taxila (Cunningham, ib. Pl. II. 8) with curvilinear swastika, to r. of tree.   Other single-die coins which are believed to be earlier than the double-die coins are described by Smith, some bearing the swastika.   No. 30 is a cast circular coin of Taxila with curvilinear swastika as type (Cunningham, ib. Pl. II. 19), ascribed by Smith to the same period as the preceding Taxilan coins (*op. cit.*, p. 159, n. 38).   No. 31 is a Tribal coin of Mahārājā Amoghabhūta, Rājā of the Kunindas, Second Century B. C. (Smith, ib. Pl. XX. 11, and Cunningham, ib. pl. V. 1).   The swastika, rectangular, and turning to r., is to the left of the *chaitya*, and above the triangular-shaped symbol. No. 32 is a later coin of Taxila (Cunningham, Coins of Mediaeval India, Pl. I. 1) issued by the Western Satraps of Mālwā and Gujurat.   To the left of the tree is a swastika.   Nos. 33 and 34 are coins which Cunningham assigns to Ujjain, but Smith to the country or territory, Avanti, in Northern India, of which Ujjain was the principal city (Smith, ib. p. 145 and 152, note 1).   No. 33 is a square copper piece (Cunningham, Ancient India, Pl. X. 5, and Smith ib. p. 152, no. 2), on the reverse of which is the so-called Ujjain or Mālava (cf. Smith, p. 145) symbol, Fig. 50a, an equilateral cross with arms terminating in circles in each of which is a swastika.   No. 34 is a copper of the same locality with Ujjain symbol as type, in the circles of which the swastika alternates

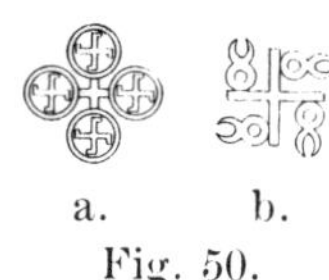

a.   b.
Fig. 50.

with the 'Taurine symbol' (Cunningham, ib. Pl. X. 7).   No. 35 is another coin assigned to Ujjain (Cunningham, *op. cit.*, Pl. X. 11).   One should compare also a large square cast copper coin figured by Smith, Pl. XXII. 19, for the swastika above a humped bull.   No. 36 is a rectangular cast copper coin assigned by Cunningham, ib. Pl. XI. 20, to Eraṇ, or Erakaina, and classed by Smith, ib. p. 202, no. 37, among the unassigned coins of Northern India of early date.   The bent arms of this swastika, Fig. 50b, are composed of the 'Taurine symbol.'   No. 37 shows a swastika turning to l., partly curvilinear, above the ' Taurine symbol,' also assigned to Eraṇ (Cunningham, Pl. XI. 15).   All of the coins assigned by Cunningham to Eran would be given by Smith to the country Avanti generally rather than to a particular city.   There are many more examples of the symbol on Indian coins.   Some of the latest which we have noticed are those on coins of the Andhras, Gautamīputra II (Cunningham, Ancient India, Pl. XII. 6) struck about the middle of the Second Century A. D., and on coins of Akbar, 963-1014 A. D. (W. H. Valentine, The Copper Coins of India, Pl. 67. 9 and Pl. 111. 150, and H. N. Wright, Cat. of the Coins of the Indian Museum, Calcutta, vol. III, Pl. VI. 556).

The Triskeles (Lycian Symbol, Sicilian Symbol, etc.)

The name, triskeles, is commonly used to designate a symbol composed of three branches radiating from a circle, central boss or point, and includes both the sign composed of three human legs, Pl. XVII. 1-21, and the so-called Lycian symbol which first occurs on coins of Lycia, Pl. XVII. 22, together with its zoomorphic modifications, Pl.

XVII. 23-26. From the study of the coins and the monuments on which the triskeles is found, it becomes evident that the symbol composed of three human legs was conceived quite independently of the Lycian symbol proper, and it therefore should be distinguished from it, merely however as a different species of the same genus. Consequently the word, triskeles, is here limited to the human-leg symbol, which on account of its wide use on the coins of Sicily, and its emblematic character as a sign for the three-pointed island, the Trinakria of the Greeks, may also be termed the Sicilian symbol.

The chronology and distribution of the coins on which the triskeles (i. e. three human legs) is found, prove that this symbol is not an anthropomorphized form of the Lycian symbol, as usually regarded (Cook, Zeus, p. 304, Babelon, Traité II^2, pp. 510, 524ff.). The type on the coins of Athens, Phlious, Aigina, Melos and Macedonia, Pl. XVII. 1-4, Fig. 52, probably precedes the symbol on Lycian coins, which first appears c. 500-460 B. C. Not only priority in time, for these coins belong to the Sixth and Fifth Centuries B. C. (Athens, 594-560 B. C., Phlious and Aigina, c. 480 B. C.), constitutes a capital objection, but geographical distribution negatives such a derivation. The triskeles at Aspendos in Pamphylia, which was imitated at Selge (and later Adada) and Etenna in Pisidia, is not earlier than the three-branched sign on Lycian coins and it is not impossible, therefore, from the standpoint of chronology to derive it from the latter. But since the triskeles must long have been a familiar symbol, as is shown by its use as a shield-device on Sixth-Century black-figured vases,[1] there is no necessity of assuming dependence upon Lycia. The way the matter appears to us is that the human-leg conception is the more essentially Greek rendering of the same idea as that expressed by the Lycian symbol. There can scarcely be any doubt that both symbols are solar, and are the graphic equivalent for Empedokles' expression Ἡελίοιο ... ὠκέα γυῖα 'swift limbs of the Sun.'[2] It does not seem likely either that the Lycian symbol was suggested by the triskeles, and it should be noted that it never takes the human-leg form though zoomorphic transformations occur.

The tetraskeles is a symbol on Lycian coins, a four-branched rendering of the regular symbol. The diskeles, two branches, and monoskeles, single branch, are further modifications, B. M. C. Lycia, Pl. VI. 7, 16 and VI. 13, but the simple three-branched figure is the one which

---

[1] J. Millingen, Ancient Unedited Monuments, 1822, Pl. IV. Journ. Hell. Stud., 1891, p. 341, note 1. Cook, Zeus, p. 307, note 6.

[2] Cook, Zeus, p. 311.

survives the longest, being found on coins of Gaul and India, another illustration of the persistence of the original type, which we saw in the case of the swastika.

Besides these varieties, there are five- and six-branched symbols on Greek coins which are not combinations of five and six ' crescents ' as sometimes described, but by-forms of the Lycian symbol. This is most apparent from the coin of Macedonia, Pl. XVII. 29, on which the arms or branches are clearly not crescents but shaped exactly like the branches of the Lycian symbol.

The Triskeles on Coins

Athens, Attica, c. 594–560 B. C.

1.   Obv. Triskeles turning to r., within plain circle.
Æ didrachm.   8.11 gr.   Berlin.   Pl. XVII. 1.
Babelon, Traité II¹, Pl. XXXIII. 11.

Fig. 51.

This is one of the group of coins with varying obverse types probably forming the earliest coinage of Athens in the time of Solon. An argument cited by Babelon in favor of the attribution to Athens is the occurrence of the triskeles on lead tokens issued by the Athenian Boulē (Traité II¹, p. 717-8, note 5) cf. Fig. 51.[1]   Whether struck at Athens or some neighboring district, the coins are not later than the Sixth Century B. C.

Phlious, Phliasia, c. 500 B. C.

2.   Obv. Triskeles, turning to r. ; above, Φ.
Æ didr.   7.05 gr.   Pl. XVII. 2.
Cat. Egger XLV, 1913, Pl. XVI. 526.

3.   Similar, type to l., within plain circle.
Æ didr.   7. 21 gr.   The Hague.
Six, Num. Chron. 1888, p. 97, 3, Pl. V. 2.   Traité II¹, Pl. XXXIII. 12.

Coins of this type are very rare. Examples have been discovered in Attica (no. 3) and Arcadia (Brussels specimen, Traité II¹, 1181). The incuse is of Aiginetic type, and the weight is Euboic-Attic. From the coin, no. 3, with plain circle as on the coin of Athens, it might be

---

[1] From a lead token of Athenian provenance in the American Numismatic Society. This is not a Boulē ticket, but is a token of uncertain use.   cf. Postolacca, Κερμάτια συμβολικά, nos. 185, 199, 237, 255, etc. in ᾿Αθήναιον, vol. IX.

inferred that the type was imitated from the latter. Six and Babelon point out that this type may refer to the three-peaked mountain, Τρικά- ρανον, Trikaranon, which overlooks the valley in which Phlious lay, but this analogy cannot explain the ultimate origin of the symbol, any more than the three promontories of Sicily can be held to account for the Sicilian symbol. In the latter case the triskeles came to be regarded as peculiarly appropriate as an emblem of all Sicily, and on a Roman coin, Pl. XVII. 19, Trinacrus, the eponymous hero of Trinacria, holds the ' sign of Sicily ' in his hand, but the Trinacrian analogy was an after- thought and not the genesis of the symbol. This symbol, like the swas- tika, goes back to the time preceding coinage. At Phlious the type is probably an instance of borrowing. The same is undoubtedly true of the following coin.

Island of Aigina, c. 480 B. C.

4. Obv. Triskeles, turning to r., with ray-like projections from the central boss or disk.

Æ stater. 12.15 gr. London. Pl. XVII. 3.
B. M. C. Attica, Pl. XXIV. 8.

The reverse type of this coin, a unique instance in the Aiginetic series, has been explained as due to an alliance between Aigina and Phlious by Babelon, Traité II[1], p. 816. Head in the Hist. Num.[2] p. 397, remarks that the fabric differs from that of the coins of Aigina, which gives some support to the conjecture. And, the incuse of the coins of Phlious, nos. 2, 3, is of Aiginetic type, which seems again to reflect reciprocal influence in the coin-types of these two cities.

Island of Melos, c. 500–416 B. C.

5. Rev. Triskeles, turning to r., ΜΑΛΙC[N] between the limbs ; within dotted circle.

Æ didr. (c. 14.00 gr. From an electrotype in the Brit. Mus.). Pl. XVII. 4.

This coin is from the Melos find described by R. Jameson in the Rev. Num., 1908, but is not the specimen illustrated, nor yet the Brit- ish Museum example from the same find, Num. Chron. 1914, Pl. VII. 15. The Jameson coin, Cat. R. Jameson, Pl. LXVI. 1299, with inscrip- tion ΜΑΛΙ[ΟΝ] which the owner dates c. 460 B. C. is evidently later than another example in the same collection, *op. cit.*, Pl. LXVI. 1287, and than the present specimen and the one in the Brit. Museum which lat- ter has the complete inscription ΜΑΛΙCΝ.

The Derrones, Thraco-Macedonian Tribe, c. 500 B. C.

6. Rev. Triskeles, turning to r., palmettes between the limbs.
Æ octodr. or dekadr. c. 40.00 gr. Fig. 52.
cf. Babelon, Traité II¹, Pl. XLIV. 6, 8, 9, and B. M. C. Macedonia, p. 150, no. 1.

Fig. 52.

Akanthos, Macedonia, c. 500–424 B. C.

7. Rev. Triskeles, turning to l., in circular incuse.
Æ tetrobol. 2.72 gr. Paris.
Babelon, Traité II¹, Pl. LIV. 7. Another example, ib. Pl. LIV. 8, has type to r.

Aspendos, Pamphylia, c. 500–400 B. C.

8. Rev. Triskeles, turning to l.
Æ stater. 10.79 gr. London. Pl. XVII. 5.
B. M. C. Lycia, Pl. XIX. 2.

9. Rev. Triskeles, turning to r. ; behind, a lion to r.
Æ stater. 10.58 gr. London. Pl. XVII. 6.
B. M. C. Lycia, Pl. XIX. 6.
10. Rev. Slinger to r. ; in r. field, triskeles, turning to l.
Æ stater. 10.88 gr. London. Pl. XVII. 7.
B. M. C. Lycia, Pl. XX. 1.

Selge, Pisidia,[1] c. 300–200 B. C.

11. Rev. Triskeles with winged feet, turning to l. (Overstruck on example
with Athena-head reverse.)
Æ 13mm. London. Pl. XVII. 8.
B. M. C. Lycia, Pl. XL. 12.

12. Rev. Triskeles, turning to l., within dotted circle.
Æ 13mm. London. Pl. XVII. 9.
B. M. C. Lycia, no. 58.

[1] Fourth-Century coins of Selge with types borrowed from Aspendos, wrestlers and slinger,
show the triskeles in the field. Etenna in Pisidia also issued staters of the Aspendos-Selge class
with the symbol, Fourth Century B. C. (B. M. C. Lycia, p. cxix).

Adada, Pisidia, First Century B. C.

13. Rev. Triskeles, turning to l., within dotted circle.
Æ 11mm. London.
B. M. C. Lycia, Pl. XXX. 2. Another coin with type to r., ibid. Pl. XXX. 3.

Latium with Campania. Central Italian Communities

Uncertain Mint, c. 300 B. C.

14. Rev. Triskeles, turning to l. ; three dots between the legs (mark of denomination).
Æ quadrans. 44mm. 80.87 gr. London.
B. M. C. Italy, p. 57, no. 17. cf. Garrucci, ib. Pl. XLV. 4. Haeberlin, ib. Pl. 67. 7–9.

Suessa Aurunca, Campania, Third Century B. C.

15. Obv. Head of Apollo r. laur. ; behind, triskeles, turning to r.
B. M. C. Italy, p. 123, no. 1. Carelli, N. I. V. T. p. 17, Pl. 64. 7.

Hierapytna, Crete, c. 400–350 B. C.

16. Obv. Triskeles, turning to r., IP | AΓ | V between the legs ; within laurel wreath.
a) Æ stater. 11.31 gr. (formerly Imhoof-Blumer).
Svoronos, Numismatique de la Crète Ancienne, Pl. XVII. 6. Imhoof-Blumer, Beiträge etc.. Zeit. f. Num. 1885, p. 133, no. 14, Pl. IV. 8.

b) 11.56 gr. Berlin.
Zeit. f. Num. XXI. 1898, p. 215, Pl. V. 2.

The triskeles does not occur elsewhere in Crete. Its appearance on a Cretan coin, an isolated instance, is precisely the same phenomenon which was presented by the swastika. This also we found here and there in widely separated regions, without trace of influence of one center upon another, a phenomenon explicable only upon the theory that the symbol was once the common property of all Greek lands. The epigram of Dioskourides cited by Cook (Zeus, p. 307) relates to a Cretan warrior and his shield-device consisting of the triskeles and Gorgoneion combined, a type which we shall soon describe on coins of Panormos.

Syracuse, Sicily, c. 345–317 B. C.

17. Rev. Triskeles, turning to r., in the center, a Gorgon's head ; within plain circle. (Obv. Head of Zeus Eleutherios.)
a) Æ 18mm. Newell. Pl. XVII. 10.

b) Similar, type to l. Glasgow.
Macdonald, Cat. Hunter. Coll. I. p. 238, no. 159, Pl. XVII. 15.

Syracuse, Sicily, Coinage of Agathokles, 317–310 B. C.

18.   Rev. Triskeles, turning to l., feet winged ; in the center a Gorgon's head within plain circle.

a) Æ dr.   4.02 gr.   Berlin.   Pl. XVII. 11.

Hill, Sicily, Pl. XI. 10.   Imhoof-Blumer, Monn. gr., p. 32, no. 73, Pl. B. 23.

b) 3.84 gr. London.

B. M. C. Sicily, p. 193, no. 353.   Head, Syracuse, Pl. VIII. 7.

c) Æ 18mm.   London.

B. M. C. Sicily, p. 193, no. 354.   Head, Syracuse, Pl. VIII. 8.

Besides the Syracusan issues with the name of the city; silver tetradrachm, Pl. XVII. 12, the first coinage of Agathokles, and later issues described in Num. Chron. 1912 (Agathokles and the Coinage of Magna Graecia) with the triskeles as symbol (num.), coins of Velia, Pl. XVII. 13, and also Terina and Metapontum show the symbol, a sign of the influence of Agathokles on coinages outside of Sicily.

Kaulonia, Italy, c. 500 B. C.

19.   Obv. Triskeles, turning to r., within dotted circle.

Æ tritemorion.   0.49 gr.   London.   Pl. XVII. 14.

B. M. C. Italy, p. 336, no. 16, fig.   Babelon, Traité II¹, Pl. LXXI. 7.

This type at Kaulonia has nothing to do with the type at Syracuse, for it was struck before 480 B. C.

Panormos, Sicily, After c. 254 B. C.

20.   Rev. Triskeles, turning to r. ; in center, a Gorgon's head ; between the legs, ears of corn.

Æ 22mm.   London.   Pl. XVII. 15.

B. M. C. Sicily, p. 122, no. 11.

Panormos, Sicily, Imperial (Augustus)

21.   Similar ; Gorgon's head winged.

Æ 25mm.   London.   Pl. XVII. 16.

B. M. C. Sicily, p. 122, no. 42.

Iaita, Sicily, After c. 241 B. C.

22.   Similar.

Æ 22mm.   London.   Pl. XVII. 17.

B. M. C. Sicily, p. 85, no. 1.

The Sicilian Symbol on Roman Coins

L. Cornelius Crus and C. Claudius Marcellus, 49 B. C.

23.   Similar.

Æ denarius.   London.   Pl. XVII. 18.

B. M. C. Coins of the Roman Republic, II, p. 558, no. 1, Pl. CXX. 3.

The reverse type of this denarius, undoubtedly derived from that of the preceding coins of Panormos and Iaita, has reference to Sicilian events, to wit, the successes of the Marcelli. Other Roman coins bear allusion by the simple triskeles to the military exploits of this same *gens* in Sicily, B. M. C. Rome, I. p. 236, a Roman As of 89 B. C., and ibid. p. 567, no. 4206, Pl. LV. 16, a denarius of 42 B. C. of the moneyer Marcellinus with the head of M. Cl. Marcellus, so that the Sicilian symbol was appropriated to become the special badge of the Marcella *gens*.

A. Allienus, *Proconsul of Sicily, 47 B. C.*

24. Rev. Trinacrus, son of Neptunus standing l., r. foot on prow; in r. hand he holds the triskeles.

Æ denarius. London. Pl. XVII. 19.

B. M. C. Rome II, p. 559, no. 5. Pl. CXX. 4. Hill, Sicily, p. 224, Pl. XV. 5.

Trinacrus, the eponymous hero of Trinacria, as Sicily was sometimes called, is here holding the symbol of Sicily, as he stands in a pose modelled after that of Neptune.

L. Aquillius Florus, *20 B. C.*

25. Rev. Triskeles, turning to r., feet winged; in center, a Gorgon's head with wings.

N aureus. London. Pl. XVII. 20.

B. M. C. ib. II, p. 67, no. 4542, Pl. LXVI. 16.

Here the Sicilian symbol relates to the successes of M'. Aquillius in 101 B. C.

Ebora Cerialis (or Castulo), The Turduli. Hispania Baetica, Second Century B. C.

26. Rev. Triskeles, turning to r., the center of which is a human head facing.

Æ 29mm. Glasgow. Pl. XVII. 21.

Macdonald, Cat. Hunter. Coll. III, p. 638, no. 6, Pl. XCVII. 15.

Fig. 53.

Gaul, Veliocasses, Third Century B. C.

27. Obv. Human figure running l., resembling triskeles below the waist.

N stater. Fig. 53.

A. Blanchet, Traité des monn. gauloises, p. 339, fig. 282.

This seems to be the triskeles 'come to life' in complete human form. It is described as 'un personnage courant,' but the lower half of the figure is designed in a perfect triskeles scheme, so that this running figure type seems to have been influenced by the triskeles.

The Lycian Symbol on Coins
Lycia, c. 500–460 B. C.

1.   Obv. Boar to l. on which symbol; above and below, symbols.   Rev. Three-branched symbol, turning to l.; in l. field, ankh, Fig. 71. 4.
Æ tetrobol.   2.90 gr.   Pl. XIX. 25.
Cat. Hirsch XXVI, Pl. XVIII. 547.
This is a very rare coin not in the B. M. C.

Aperlae, Lycia, c. 480–460 B. C.
2.   Rev. Three-branched symbol, turning to l.
Æ stater.   9.63 gr.   London.   Pl. XVII. 22.
B. M. C. Lycia, Pl. III. 7.

Kuprlle, Dynast of Lycia, c. 480–450 B. C.
3.   Rev. Similar symbol, turning to l., one branch ending in the head of a monster (griffin?).
Æ stater.   9.54 gr.   London.   Pl. XVII. 23.
B. M. C. Lycia, Pl. III. 14.

4.   Rev. Similar, turning to r., branches ending in swan's heads.
Æ stater.   10.85 gr.   Paris.   Pl. XVII. 24.
Babelon, Traité II¹, Pl. XCVI. 5.   B. M. C. Lycia, Pl. XLIV. 5.

Tänägurä, Dynast of Lycia, c. 450–420 B. C.
5.   Rev. Similar, turning to r., one branch at least ending in a serpent's head.
Æ stater.   8.63 gr.   London. Pl. XVII. 25.
B. M. C. Lycia, Pl. V. 3.

Uncertain Dynast of Lycia, Thiban (?), c. 480 B. C.
6.   Rev. Similar, turning to r., branches ending in cock's heads.
Æ stater.   9.27 gr.   London.   Pl. XVII. 26.
B. M. C. Lycia, Pl. III. 2.

Täththiväibi, Dynast of Lycia, c. 480–460 B. C.
7.   Rev. Four-branched symbol, turning to l.
Æ stater.   9.91 gr.   London.   Pl. XVII. 27.
B. M. C. Lycia, Pl. V. 9.

Khäriga, Dynast of Lycia, c. 410 B. C.
8.   Rev. Four-branched symbol, turning to r.; in the inner ring, owl to l.
Æ drachm.   3.11 gr.   London.   Pl. XVII. 28.
B. M. C. Lycia, Pl. VI. 6.

Olba, Cilicia. Ajax, High-Priest of Olba, and Governor of Lalassis and Kennatis
10/11–14/15 A. D.

9.   Rev. Lycian symbol, with central circle represented by a mere point, turning
to l.

Æ 24mm.   London.
B. M. C. Cilicia, Pl. XXI. 8.

The presence of the Lycian symbol on the coin no. 9 is explained in
the B. M. C. p. liii by the fact that the symbol is found carved in the
rock at several places in this district, valuable evidence of the spread
of the symbol into Cilicia.   On the Lycian coinage the symbol does not
occur after c. 350 B. C., but in the modified form of the preceding coin
with central circle dwindled to a mere point, it is found also at Megara
and in Macedonia.

Megara, Megaris, c. 400–350 B. C.

10.   Rev. Five-branched symbol, turning to l.
Æ.   3.24 gr.   Pl. XVII. 30.
cf. B. M. C. Attica, Pl. XXI. 2.

11.   Rev. Three-branched symbol, turning to r.
Æ.   1.56 gr. (formerly Prowe).   Pl. XVII. 31.
Cat. Prowe, Egger XL, Pl. XVIII. 990.   cf. B. M. C. Attica, Pl. XXI. 3.

Amphaxitis, District of Macedonia, c. 185–168 B. C.

12.   Obv. Macedonian shield bearing as central device a six-branched symbol,
turning to l., enclosed in a double plain circle ; the same device repeated, within crescents or incomplete circles, in the space surrounding the central circle.
Æ tetradrachm.   16.71 gr.   Pl. XVII. 29.

The type of the Megarian coin, no. 10, is usually described as composed of five crescents, but in view of the three-branched type, no. 11,
which is reasonably interpreted as the Lycian symbol from the analogy
of the coin of Olba, no. 9, there can be no doubt that this type and the
analogous six-branched device on the Macedonian coin, no. 12, are
derivations of the Lycian symbol.   In fact on the latter piece the
branches are most distinctly reminiscent of the Lycian symbol, and are
plainly not crescents.   Again, on the coinage of Macedonia *in Genere*,
c. 158-146 B. C. (B. M. C. Macedonia, no. 17), the regular three-
branched sign occurs on the shield type, showing that the Lycian symbol had made its way into Macedonia as into Megaris.   Indeed it had
penetrated to northern Asia Minor in the Fourth Century, coins of
Abydos, Birytis, Neandria and Rhoiteion (B. M. C. Troas, Pl. I. 8,
VIII. 5; Inv. Wadd. in Rev. Num. 1897, no. 1192 and Traité II², Pl.

CLXVII. 9) in Troas, and of Thebe in Mysia (B. M. C. Mysia, p. 179), showing the three-branched or standard form of the sign, all of the period c. 400-300 B. C. At Argos in Peloponnesus it is also found (B. M. C. Peloponnesus, p. 140) at the same period. This symbol, therefore, which started as a local device, and had an intensive local use, spread to a considerable distance from the point which may be designated its home-place. It is probable that the following Gaulish coin-type was not independently conceived, but derived indirectly from the Lycian symbol.

Boii, Tribe of Gaul, Third to Second Century B. C.

13.   Obv. Three-branched symbol, with well-defined circle and central point, turning to r.

N stater.   7.35 gr. (formerly E. F. Weber).   Pl. XVII. 32.

Cat. Weber, Hirsch XXI, Pl. I. 160.

A symbol called 'triskeles,' and of the Lycian form occurs also on coins of India, anonymous cast circular copper of Northern India, probably issued before 200 A. D. (Cunningham, Coins of Ancient India, Pl. I. 26, horned bull to r., above, symbol, V. A. Smith, *op. cit.*, p. 202, no. 9). Whether this sign goes back to the Lycian symbol or not is hard to say, but the history of the swastika favors such an assumption. The latter symbol, as we saw, after a life of a millenium or two in Greek lands was adopted as a vital symbol in Indian religion, and was correspondingly reflected on the coinage. The Lycian symbol also, we suspect, had a use much wider than we can now postulate from the monuments extant. It would of course be readily accepted in a land where religious sentiment was especially prone to symbolism. The cast copper coin here illustrated, Fig. 54, from India, locality unknown

Fig. 54.

to the writer, bears a type suggestive of the four-branched Lycian symbol, though here the arms take a double curve. The central circle and point are clearly defined, however, and the sign is more like the Lycian than an exceptionally curving swastika which some may prefer to call it.

The Lycian symbol, of three or four branches, occurs further as countermark on the punchmarked Persian sigloi which had circulated in Lycia, Cilicia and Cyprus (Newell, A Cilician Find, Num. Chron. 1914, pp. 23ff., and Fig. 1, nos. 17, 34), and on a coin of Aspendos, B. M. C. Lycia, Pl. XXI. 8.

In conclusion, we should not omit the rather remarkable, though well-known survival of the human-leg triskeles on the coinage of the Isle of man (from the Seventeenth Century on), derived from the Sicilian triskeles, Fig. 55 (Num. Chron. 1899, pp. 35ff.).

Fig. 55.

The introduction of the symbol into the Isle of Man is generally supposed to have been effected by Alexander III of Scotland, King of Man and the Isles, 1266-1286, whose wife was the sister of the Queen of Sicily. From its use on the arms of the Isle, where the earliest examples show the legs unclothed, it passed to the coinage where it is always armor-clad and spurred.

The Significance of the Swastika, Triskeles, etc.

It has been indicated at several points in the foregoing description that the swastika is most commonly regarded as a solar sign, that its form has been interpreted as signifying the rotary motion of the sun. This is the theory of L. Müller and also that of P. Gardner and E. Thomas. The latter gives the same meaning to the triskeles and Lycian symbol which are analogous 'turning' emblems, and expresses his interpretation as follows: " As far as I have been able to trace or connect the various manifestations of this emblem, they one and all resolve themselves into the primitive conception of solar motion, which was intuitively associated with the rolling or wheel-like projection of the sun through the upper or visible arc of the heavens, as understood and accepted in the crude astronomy of the ancients " (Num. Chron. 1880, p. 19). Many other hypotheses have been proposed to explain the swastika, most of which are reviewed in Wilson's book, but the above theory may be said to hold the field. Now, the triskeles and Lycian symbol very clearly express motion, rotary motion, and seem not ill-adapted to designate graphically the course of the sun in the heavens which, as we definitely know, the Greeks also expressed by the conception of the Sun-god in his chariot, and by the solar wheel (see especially Cook's admirable discussion in his Zeus, pp. 197ff.). For this concept, the swastika does not seem at first view quite so well suited.

And yet, it is in connection with the swastika on monuments that we get the only conclusive evidence that either of these symbols was a solar sign. These bits of evidence have all been noted in turn, aud we shall dwell again here only on that presented by the coin of Mesembria, no. 7, Fig. 44, Pl. XVI. 6. The Greek roots of which the name of the town is composed, $\mu\acute{\epsilon}\sigma\eta + \dot{\eta}\mu\acute{\epsilon}\rho\alpha$ = 'midday,' 'noon' or 'south' seem to be literally expressed in the inscription on this coin, MEϟ + swastika, a sort of punning allusion to the name of the city. When we take into consideration the fact that this remarkable combination of legend + symbol, an expression to render the ethnic, occurs on a wheel type,

Fig. 56.

Fig. 57.

beyond doubt solar (cf. Fig. 56 with inscription META (= MEϟϟA), and Fig. 57, a coin of Kalchedon), the meaning of the swastika as solar seems settled beyond dispute. We may then adopt this general hypothesis without hesitation. Certainly no other theory yet proposed has any support to match that which the monuments afford in favor of Müller's explanation. Particularly thin and untenable are two theories, more recently put forward than any mentioned in Wilson's book, of Mrs. Nuttall and W. Schultz, by which the swastika is derived from the constellation of Ursa Major, and from a supposed fundamental character of the 'West-Semitic' alphabet, respectively.[1] For the sake of completeness, we may mention again that Figs. 21, 22, 23 and 30, together with the Mesembrian coin, present satisfactory proof of the solar meaning of the sign among the Greeks, Figs. 21 and 30, as clearly as could be desired. In China, we have the absolute equivalence of the sign for the 'sun' (p. 143). In America and India, inferences may be drawn from the association of the swastika with other signs, e. g. in bead-work (Wilson, *op. cit.*, Pl. XV), and in the stone carving, Fig. 41, but this argument has an obvious weakness, and should not be pressed. In the sandpoint drawing (Wilson, *op. cit.*, Pl. 17) the swastika is brought into close connection with the cardinal points, and this drawing suggests an original solar meaning to some, but to others an original use of the sign in America to denote the four points of the compass.

[1] Add to the bibliography on pp. 115ff., W. R. Harris' article on the swastika in America, in Annual Arch. Report of the Ontario Prov. Mus., Toronto, 1914, pp. 26–43.

Interesting arguments have recently been advanced by Cook (Zeus, pp. 472ff.) to show that the earliest form of the Cretan Labyrinth was a swastika design, and that the Labyrinth was originally the place where a mimetic solar dance was performed. Coins of Knossos, Figs.

Fig. 58.

Fig. 59.

Fig. 60.

58-60, show how the swastika-Labyrinth (Figs. 58, 59) developed into a maze (Fig. 60). The thesis proposed by Cook that the Labyrinth was a dancing-ground or *orchéstra* of solar pattern whereon the Minotaur, impersonated by the crown-prince of Knossos, performed a ritual solar dance, forms a fascinating chapter in this learned work, and, if accepted by scholars, would lend great strength to the solar meaning of

Fig. 61.

Fig. 62.

the sign. Whether we should follow his tentative suggestion that the so-called Gaza sign, Figs. 61 and 62, on coins of this city is also a swastika-like design bearing some relation, though distant, to the Cretan Labyrinth, is perhaps more debatable. Sir Arthur Evans had already

Fig. 63.

Fig. 64.

noted the resemblance of the Knossian Labyrinth on coins and the peculiar sign on the coins of Gaza (Minoa) to the Minoan swastika (Annual of the Brit. School at Athens, IX, pp. 88ff.). Less probable seems to us Cook's suggestion that the maeander design on coins of

Magnesia ad Maeandrum, Antiocheia ad Maeandrum, etc., Figs. 63, 64, have aught to do with the Labyrinth. The pattern under Apollo's figure on the coin of Magnesia is a fully-developed maeander, which pattern may have grown out of the swastika, a supposition incapable of proof,[1] but on these coins has clearly only the punning allusion to the ' meandering river.'

Investigators have frequently sought to derive the swastika figure from the solar wheel (Cook, pp.336-7, note 1, and Déchelette, Manuel II[1], pp. 453ff.), but though the solar wheel is very ancient, being found in Minoan art on a steatite mold from Crete (Déchelette, ib. Fig. 191; Dussaud, *op. cit.*, Fig. 289, cf. Fig. 288) there is no connecting link between it and the swastika. W. H. Ward in his Seal Cylinders of Western Asia, p. 394, hints that the swastika figure may be possibly derived from the ' Kassite ' cross, but, if this were so, we should expect to find it on Syro-Hittite cylinders, whereas it is never there found. An equal-armed cross might have been the graphic basis of the sign, to which were added the arms, the ultimately original conception being that of a graphic picture of the four points of the compass. This suggestion has been made by several writers, and of all the hypotheses which have been formed to reach back to the basic concept for the figure, this seems the most probable to us. The figure may then have been felt to be appropriate as a picture of something revolving, and consequently employed as a graphic representation of the revolving sun. If we should care to use the argument from association, we might turn to account the two Trojan vases with the swastika and cross cantonnée, a most natural picture of the cardinal points, in an identical position on both Figs. 2 and 3; and also the four points sometimes found in conjunction with the swastika (p. 128).

So much for speculation concerning the origin of the figure. The meaning at least is tolerably clear. For the Lycian symbol we have no such direct evidence that the sign was solar.[2] But indirect proofs are the following. A constant type on the Lycian coinage, after the sym-

---

[1] The coins of Knossos shown by Cook, Figs. 333–338, seem to favor this derivation, but the maeander, like the swastika, was much more ancient than these coins. It is obvious, at any rate, that the contrary proposition that the swastika is ꞏ strictly speaking, to be regarded as a fragmentary piece of maeander ' (H. B. Walters, History of Greek Pottery II, p. 214) is untrue.

[2] It has been maintained that the zoomorphic types of the Lycian symbol, with cock's heads, swan's heads and a serpent's head may be taken as proof of the solar meaning. Also, that the triskeles superimposed upon an eagle and a lion on coins of Aspendos shows the like association with solar animals. It does not seem improbable that all of these types have a solar connotation, but it would be impossible to go into the evidence at this point.

bol ceased to be used, is the head of Apollo or Helios, god of light. The symbol of the same meaning as the Lycian, the triskeles, or human-leg figure on the coins of Hispania, Pl. XVII. 21, is modified by the introduction of a human face which suggests an anthropomorphized solar disk. This interpretation of the Hispanic emblem is made more probable by the occurrence of this same device on a Punic stele (cited by Cook, *op. cit.*, p. 308, Fig. 406, here Fig. 65 and noted also by Goblet

Fig. 65.

d'Alviella, *op. cit.*, p. 54) dedicated to Ba' al Hamman, a sky-god or sun-god, where, Cook conjectures, it may be a special sign of ' Lord Ba' al, the sun-god ' of the inscription.

As regards the origin of the figure (not the concept) of the triskeles, it had long seemed to the writer quite possible to derive it from the figure presented by tumblers, who, in pairs, with bodies locked, by turning over and over, give the visual impression of the triskeles to the onlooker. This idea was first conceived when, after a sojourn in Sicily where the Panormite type is quite commonly seen on post-cards, the writer witnessed in Paris just such an acrobatic performance as here described. The conclusion that this was indeed the living triskeles was irresistible. Since that experience, the passage in Plato's Symposium, 189D-190C[1], was re-read, in which a reference to this illusion created by tumblers is made in the following words: " When he

---

[1] Quoted by Cook, Zeus, p. 310, in support of his theory about the Kyklopes and their connection with the Lycian symbol,

started to run fast, he looked like tumblers who bring their legs round so as to point upwards and tumble along in a circle." This passage is a verbal picture of what the writer had witnessed, and since the word-picture of Plato is as valuable as a vase-painting of this acrobatic feat would be, it still seems a reasonable conclusion that the triskeles as a figure might have been thus derived. It remains finally to point out that the central disk or circle in both the triskeles and Lycian symbol may stand for the sun's orb.

In conclusion we may cite the two figures given by Hein (*op. cit.*, Figs. 9, 30), the one, Fig. 66, said to be the Mexican hieroglyph for the

Fig. 66.

Fig. 67.

concept 'year,' and the other, Fig. 67, the Aztec hieroglyph for 'time.' These signs are strongly reminiscent of the swastika and triskeles and enable us to see exactly how such figures were evolved to express a primitive concept. We shall reserve the discussion of the psychological significance of these symbols, as well as the two following, the ankh and the winged disk, for the concluding chapter of this paper.

THE ANKH

The ankh[1] is an Egyptian symbol which was at the same time a hieroglyph in the Egyptian writing-system, having the meaning of ' life ' or ' to live ' (serving also as a determinative in the highly complex system of expression which the Egyptians evolved). Its antiquity as a symbol is very great, but just when it is first seen in a symbolic usage on the monuments would be a matter for Egyptologists to decide. It is very common as a symbol on monuments of the Empire, c. 1580-945 B. C., two of which from the Metropolitan Museum, New York, are here illustrated on Pl. XVIII. 1, 3, while a monument of the Thirtieth Dynasty, c. 382-364 B. C., also in the New York Museum, is

---

[1] For bibliography consult Goblet d'Alviella, *op. cit.* The chief article is by D. Raoul-Rochette, Memoires de l'Académie des Inscriptions et Belles-Lettres, vol. XVII.

figured on Pl. XVIII. 2. On the first of these, Pl. XVIII. 1, a relief[1] from a memorial temple of Rameses I at Abydos, Nineteenth Dynasty, Reigns of Rameses I and Seti I, c. 1315-1292 B. C., the ankh, Fig. 71. 1, may be seen among the hieroglyphs above, and also as a symbol equipped with two human arms in the lower part of the relief. The subjects of this relief are two, that in the left section represents Seti I making offerings before the ' symbol of Abydos ' to the right of which is the god Osiris, holding the ankh by the ' ring ' in his left hand. The ankh is seen here personified as supporter of staves holding up images of the sacred cow to right and to left of the ' symbol of Abydos.' The right section has a similar representation with the goddess Isis receiving offerings from Rameses I at the ' symbol of Abydos.' Fig. XVIII. 3 is a small pylon-shaped pectoral of glazed steatite, Nineteenth to Twentieth Dynasty, c. 1300-1100 B. C.,[2] a fragment with uncertain representation, showing however the goddess Isis recognizable by her head-dress of solar disk between bull's horns and uraeus-snakes, holding an ankh in each hand, one by the handle, or upright, and one by the ring.

Another monument of the same period is the large relief[3] from the same temple as that of Pl. XVIII. 1, showing Rameses I seated before food-offerings, while below Nile-gods bring gifts, and at the right priests perform the ceremonies of the offering-ritual. Rameses I here holds the ankh by the ring in his right hand. It is seen also below the ' tet ' sign in the lower register.

Another splendid illustration of the ankh in the New York Museum is a window from a palace of the period of the Empire,[4] showing the ankh, a foot high at least, with the ' tet ' sign on either side, and to right and left, the scarab surmounted by a solar disk, and the ' Was ' scepter, while in the upper section are similar scarabs and hawks. A particularly interesting example in the Museum is an ankh of large size,[5] which was found in a coffin, here seen amidst staves and scepters, from a burial of the Twelfth Dynasty, c. 2000 B. C. The symbol is frequently found together with the sandals lying at the feet of the dead.

The symbol is of frequent occurrence on scarabs. Fig. 68. 1-5, shows a number of them from the collection of Mr. Newell, with the ankh as symbolic sign.

[1] In the Eleventh Egyptian room, side-wall.

[2] Eleventh Egyptian room, wall-case, (about actual size).

[3] Eleventh Egyptian room, side-wall.

[4] Twelfth Egyptian room.   [5] Sixth Egyptian room.

From Egyptian the sign passed into Assyrian art at the time of the invasion of the Eighteenth Dynasty. Seal cylinders of the Syro-Hittite class figured in Ward's book give many illustrations. Three

1 2 3 4 5

Fig. 68.

seals from the collection of Mr. Newell, Fig. 69. 1-3, are of this class. Fig. 69. 3, is illustrated and described by Ward, ib. Fig. 941.

The symbol does not appear to have been the exclusive attribute of any one god, since it is found on the monuments in the hands of various gods, Amen-Ra, Kneph, Isis, Hathor, Osiris etc., and of kings. Frequently it is held out towards the living as a sign of vital power,

1

2   3

Fig. 69.

and is offered to the dead as a token of resurrection. It is therefore a sign of immortality as well as of life, two meanings which almost blend. One of the most interesting of all the monuments bearing the symbol is a bas-relief on the wall of a temple at Luxor, described as follows by S. Sharpe, Egyptian Mythology, London, 1863, p. 17, Fig. 28. The scene represents the birth of a king. The first section shows the god Thoth with ibis-head, with ink and pen-cone in hand as a messenger of the gods, announcing to the maiden queen Mutemua, that she is about to give birth to a son who is to be king Amenhotep III. In the second section Kneph, a spirit, with the ram's head, and the goddess Hathor both take hold of the queen by her hands and place in her mouth the ankh symbol, sign of life. In the third section, the queen, about to give birth to the child, is seated on the midwife's stool; two of the attendants rub her hands to ease her pains, while another holds up the new-born babe over which is written the name of the king Amenhotep III. He holds his finger to his mouth to mark his infancy; he has not yet learned to speak. Lastly, several gods or priests attend in adoration upon their knees to present gifts to the child. In this picture we have the Annunciation, Conception, Birth and Adoration, just as described in the first and second chapters of Luke, and so often depicted in religious painting. Here the ankh, itself a life symbol, has a meaning which may justly be described as phallic, though as our conclusion will indicate, it is better to restrict this interpretation rigidly to such a use as that just shown, and to interpret this symbol in the general way which will be analyzed in our concluding chapter.

Fig. 70.

Like the swastika the ankh was adopted by the Christians probably as another 'cross' symbol.[1] Fig. 70 shows a church tapestry (restored)[2] of the Christian period about the Fifth Century, which is covered with figures of the ankh and the equal-armed cross. Above in the lunette the ankh is seen with the Christ-monogram enclosed in the 'ring' of

[1] Champollion gave the sign the name, crux ansata or cross with a handle, by which it is frequently known.

[2] K. M. Kaufmann, Handbuch der christlichen Archäologie, Fig. 236.

the symbol. This figure is taken from Kaufmann's Handbuch in which may be found many other instances of the use of the ankh in Christian times, graffiti from the Christian necropolis of the Oasis in the Libyan desert, Roman and Gallic sarcophagi of Christians, embroidered grave-garments from Egypt.

A most instructive side-light on the Christian attitude towards the symbol, which proves that they accepted it as they did the swastika, as a 'cross' symbol, is the anecdote related by Sozomen, Hist. Eccles. VII. 15, p. 725B. The temple of Dionysos at Alexandria was converted by the Christians into a church, and in order to cast contumely on the pagan mysteries, a mock procession, including a phallephoria, was held. Thereupon the pagans were enraged and tortured the Christians. The Christians became angry and seized the Serapeum. The Emperor Arcadius sided with the Christians. During the demolition of the Serapeum, it was said that stones were found on which were discovered hieroglyphic characters in the *form of a cross*, which upon being submitted to the inspection of the learned were declared to be signs meaning *the life to come*. This discovery was responsible for many conversions among the people who saw in the signs a prophetic allusion to the redemption.

The priests then evidently told the people of Alexandria that the ankh sign meant immortality, and the Christians were struck by this non-pagan concept, and could readily regard the Egyptian 'cross' sign, as a mysterious forerunner of their own sacred symbol.

The ankh is most familiar to students of Greek numismatics in the coinages of Cyprus and Cilicia, Pl. XIX. 4-11, and 12-24. It occurs also on coins struck in Lycia, Pl. XIX. 25-27, and Phoenicia, Pl. XIX. 28-31, and Fig. 73; also on a coin of Syria, Fig. 72. The following is a description of the principal types showing the different varieties of the ankh, Fig. 71. 2-10.

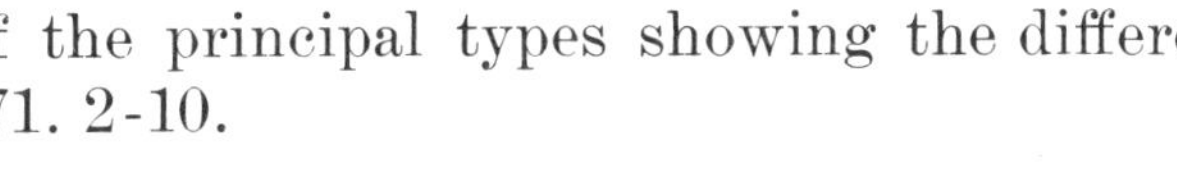

Fig. 71.

The Ankh on Greek Coins

Uncertain of Caria (?), Kaunos (?), Sixth Century B. C.

1. Obv. Forepart of lioness to l.; on shoulder, slanting ankh, Fig. 71. 5.

Æ stater. c. 11.00 gr. (formerly Duruflé). Pl. XIX. 1.

Cat. Duruflé, Rollin et Feuardent, May, 1910, Pl. XII. 556. cf. B. M. C. Caria, p. xliv. Head, H. N.[2] p. 612, suggests Kaunos on the Carian coast opposite Rhodes as the possible mint-place.

2. Similar type, but later style ; on shoulder, ankh, Fig. 71. 4.
Æ stater. 11.06 gr. Berlin. Pl. XIX. 2.
Dressel, Zeitschrift f. Num. XXII. (1900) Pl. VIII. 20.

3. Similar, with ankh, Fig. 71. 8.
Æ stater. 11.17 gr. Paris. Pl. XIX. 3.
Babelon, Traité II¹, Pl. XIX. 22.

This group of coins belongs to an undetermined country. From
the reverse which is a peculiar form of incuse, a square divided horizontally by a broad band, met with only on the coins of Poseidion in Caria
and of Lindos and Kameiros in Rhodes, an island off the coast of Caria,
these coins have been conjecturally attributed to Caria. It should be
noted however that the ankh is not found on Carian or Rhodian coins.
Other staters belonging to the same group are nos. 15, 16, 18, 20 of Pl.
XIX in the Traité, and two examples in sale catalogues, Cat. Burel,
Rollin et Feuardent, 1913, Pl. VI. 300 and Cat. Merzbacher, 1910, Pl.
XII. 722, these two latter pieces similar to no. 1 of our list, but with ○
in place of the ankh. Babelon assigns the whole group to an uncertain mint of Caria, Lycia or Pamphylia.

Salamis, Cyprus. Euelthon, c. 560–525 B. C.

4. Obv. Ram lying to l. ; in front, ankh, Fig. 71. 2.
Æ stater. 11.12 gr. London. Pl. XIX. 4.
B. M. C. Cyprus, Pl. IX. 1.

Salamis, Cyprus. Gorgos (?), c. 480–460 B. C.

5. Rev. Ankh with ring composed of plain circle within dotted circle ; in ring,
traces of Cypriote sign, *Ku* (for Κυπρίων).
Æ stater. 10.95 gr. London. Pl. XIX. 5.
B. M. C. Cyprus, Pl. X. 4, and p. lxxxix.

6. Similar, with sign *Pa* (Ba for Βασιλέως) in ring.
Æ stater. 10.89 gr. London. Pl. XIX. 6.
B. M. C. Cyprus, Pl. X. 6.

Uncertain of Cyprus, Soli (?), c 480 B. C.

7. Ankh as above, without sign in ring.
Æ stater. 11.16 gr. London. Pl. XIX. 7.
B. M. C. Cyprus, Pl. XIII. 4.

Paphos, Cyprus, c. 480 B. C.

8. Obv. Human-headed bull kneeling to r. with head reverted ; below, ankh,
Fig. 71. 3.
Æ stater. 11.10 gr. Paris. Pl. XIX. 8.
Babelon, Traité II¹, Pl. XXVII. 7.

Paphos, Cyprus, Stasandros, c. 450 B. C.

9.   Obv. Bull standing to l. ; above, winged disk ; in front, ankh, Fig. 71. 3.
Æ stater. 10.91 gr. London. Pl. XX. 20.
B. M. C. Cyprus, Pl. VII. 13.

Kition, Cyprus, Demonikos, c. 388–387 B. C.

10.   Obv. Athena standing, holding spear and shield ; in l. field, ankh, Fig. 71. 6.
Æ stater. 10.95 gr. Paris. Pl. XIX. 9.
Babelon, Traité II², Pl. CXXXI. 12.

Kition, Cyprus, Pumiathon, c. 361–312 B. C.

11.   Obv. Herakles advancing to r., holding club and bow; in r. field, ankh,
Fig. 71. 2.
N hemi-stater. c. 4.15 gr. Newell. Pl. XIX. 10.
cf. Babelon, Traité II², Pl. CXXXI. 31.

Kurion, Cyprus, c. 400 B. C.

12.   Rev. Athena seated to l. on the beak of a prow ; in l. field, ankh, Fig. 71. 2.
Æ stater. 10.81 gr. Paris. Pl. XIX. 11.
Babelon, Perses Achéménides. Pl. XX. 10.

Uncertain of Cilicia (?), Mallos (?) or Magarsis (?), c. 450 B. C.

13.   Obv. Ram walking to l.; in front, ꜰ ; above, ankh, placed horizontally,
Fig. 71. 2.
Æ stater. 10.83 gr. The Hague.
Six, Num. Chron. 1895, Pl. VII. 17.

Tarsos, Cilicia, c. 450 B. C.

14.   Obv. King (of Cilicia ?) wearing Persian head-dress, on horseback galloping
to r.; in front, ankh, Fig. 71. 2.
Rev. Hoplite, carrying spear and shield, kneeling to r. ; behind, ankh, Fig. 71. 4.
Æ stater. 10.55 gr. Paris. Pl. XIX. 12.
Babelon, Traité II², Pl. CX. 5.

Tarsos, Cilicia, c. 440 B. C.

15.   Rev. King of Persia wearing tiara and kandys, advancing to r., holding
spear in r. hand and ankh in l., Fig. 71. 4.
Æ stater. 10.54 gr. Glasgow. Pl XIX. 13.
Macdonald, Cat. Hunter. Coll. II, Pl. LX. 5.

16.   Obv. King (of Cilicia ?) on horseback advancing to l. ; beneath horse, ankh,
Fig. 71. 4.
Æ stater. 10.64 gr. Glasgow. Pl. XIX. 14.
Id. II, Pl. LX. 6.

17. Rev. Archer wearing long chiton, kneeling to r. and shooting; in l. field, ankh, Fig. 71. 4.

Æ stater. 10.89 gr. Glasgow. Pl. XIX. 15.
Id. II, Pl. LX. 7.

18. Rev. Similar.
Æ tetrobol. 3.18 gr. London. Pl. XIX. 16.
B. M. C. Cilicia, Pl XXVIII. 11.

Tarsos, Cilicia, c. 400 B. C.

19. Obv. Battlemented walls of a city with three towers; above, seated to l. on throne, a king (of Persia) holding a spear in both hands; facing him, draped figure to r. (king of Cilicia) resting both hands on scepter; in field above, ankh, Fig. 71. 2.
Æ tetrobol. 3.33 gr. London. Pl. XIX. 17.
B. M. C. Cilicia, Pl. XXVI. 1 (attributed to Soloi, and noted as uncertain, but now regarded as belonging to Tarsos).

Soloi, Cilicia, c. 400 B. C.

20. Rev. Bunch of grapes on stalk with tendrils; in r. field, ankh, Fig. 71. 2.
Æ stater. c. 10.62 gr. Boston. Pl. XIX. 18.
Regling, Samml. Warren, Pl. XXIX. 1262.

Issos, Cilicia, c. 400 B. C.

21. Rev. Herakles standing, holding club, bow and lion's skin; in r. field, ankh, Fig. 71. 1.
Æ stater. 10.59 gr. Newell. Pl. XIX. 19.
Newell, Num. Chron. 1914, Pl. III. 1. cf. B. M. C. Cilicia, p. cxxvii.

Mallos, Cilicia, c. 425–385 B. C.

22. Rev. Swan standing to l.; behind, ankh, Fig. 71. 2.
Æ stater. c. 10.35 gr. (formerly Duruflé). Pl. XIX. 20.
Cat. Duruflé, Rollin et Feuardent, May, 1910, Pl. XIII. 587. cf. B. M. C. Cilicia, Pl. XVI. 8–12, the last specimen has a different form of the ankh from that found elsewhere, like Fig. 71. 2, with two horizontal bars.

Tarsos, Cilicia, Satrap Pharnabazos, c. 379–374 B. C.

23. Rev. Head of Ares in crested Athenian helmet to r.; in front, ankh, Fig. 71. 2.
Æ stater. 10.67 gr. London. Pl. XIX. 21.
B. M. C. Cilicia, Pl. XXIX. 4.

24. Similar, with ankh, Fig. 71. 7.
Æ stater. 9.43 gr. London. Pl. XIX. 22.
B. M. C. Cilicia, Pl. XXIX. 3.

25. Similar, head to l.; behind, ankh, Fig. 71. 7.
Æ stater. Boston (Perkins Coll. 550). Pl. XIX. 23.

Tarsos, Cilicia, Satrap Mazaios, c. 361–333 B. C.

26. Obv. Ba' altars seated on throne to l., holding ear of corn and bunch of grapes in r. and scepter in l. hand ; under throne, ankh, Fig. 71. 3.

Æ stater. 11.01 gr. London. Pl. XIX. 24.

B. M. C. Cilicia, Pl. XXX. 6.

Rhosos, Syria, Second or First Century B. C.

27. Rev. Syrian god, Ba' al or Hadad Ramman, horned, standing between two reclining bulls ; on head, ankh, Fig. 71. 2.

Æ 20mm. (formerly Imhoof-Blumer), Fig. 72.

Imhoof-Blumer, Monn. gr. p. 440, and Choix de Monnaies grecques, Pl. VII. 223.

Fig. 72.

Rhosos was situated on the Gulf of Issos and is sometimes classed among the cities of Cilicia, but is more commonly placed in Syria. This bronze coin is much later than most of the coins of Cyprus, Cilicia, Lycia and Phoenicia on which the ankh is chiefly found. After c. 300 B. C. the ankh occurs only on the Parthian and Sassanian coinages. The type of the coin is Syrian, but the symbol is probably due to the proximity of the town to Cilicia where it is so frequent.

Lycia, c. 500–460 B. C.

28. Rev. Lycian symbol and ankh, Fig. 71. 4.

Æ tetrobol. 2.90 gr. (formerly Philipsen). Pl. XIX. 25.

Cat. Philipsen, Hirsch XXVI, Pl. XVIII. 547.

This rare coin has been more fully described under the Lycian symbol, no. 1.

Lycia, Khäräi as Dynast of Xanthos, c. 450–410 B. C.

29. Rev. Head of bearded satrap in Persian head-dress to r. ; in r. field, ankh, Fig. 71. 8, inverted.

Æ stater. 8.35 gr. London. Pl. XIX. 26.

B. M. C. Lycia, Pl. VI. 2.

Tlos, Lycia, c. 400–390 B. C.

30. Rev. Two lions seated confronting, r. fore-paws raised ; between them, ankh, Fig. 71. 8, inverted.

Æ diobol. 1.34 gr. (pierced). London. Pl. XIX. 27.

B. M. C. Lycia, Pl. VIII. 3. cf. Num. Chron. 1914, Pl. II. 5 (stater with same types).

The symbol on nos. 29, 30 is the ankh inverted, as follows from the variant on coin no. 3 of our list, and the Parthian piece, no. 41. A better example of this coin-type is one of the recent acquisitions of the British Museum, Num. Chron. 1912, Pl. VII. 5, weighing 2.54 gr. and with symbol apparently like Fig. 71. 8, with horizontal bar.

Uncertain of Phoenicia(?), Sidon(?), c. 440 B. C.

31.   Rev. Ankh, Fig. 71. 4, lying diagonally within dotted incuse.   (Obv. Galley before a city-wall with two towers ; in exergue, two lions back to back.)
Æ (plated) 16mm.   Berlin.   Fig. 73.
Dressel, Zeit. f. Num. XXII, p. 253.   cf. Babelon, Traité II², Pl. CXVIII. 14, and II², no. 530bis, Fig. (a coin of Tarsos with the ankh similarly placed).

Fig. 73.

This form of the ankh is found in Cilicia frequently, and in Lycia, Pl. XIX. 25, and on coins no. 1 and 2.   The obverse type is Sidonian.

Uncertain.   Satraps of Phoenicia, Palestine and Arabia, or some mint in Cilicia
(Aigeai or Kelenderis?), c. 450–400 B. C.

32.   Rev. Owl facing, wings open ; above each wing, ankh, Fig. 71. 2.
Æ stater.   10.76 gr.   London.   Pl. XIX. 28.
B. M. C. Cilicia, Pl. IX. 12.   Babelon, Traité II², no. 1029, Fig.

Satrapal Coins of Western Asia Minor, Kyme (?), Spithridates, c. 334 B. C.

33.   Rev. Fore-part of horse to r. with ϟΓΙ ; above, ankh, Fig. 71. 4.
Æ 14mm.   London.
B. M. C. Ionia, Pl. XXXI. 12.   cf. Babelon, Traité II², Pl. LXXXIX. 4.

Byblos, Phoenicia, Enylos, c. 333 B. C.

34.   Rev, Lion devouring a bull to l. ; under the lion and also on the haunch of the bull, ankh, Fig. 71. 6.
Æ tetradrachm.   13.20 gr.   Paris.   Pl. XIX. 29.
Babelon, Traité II², Pl. CXVII. 25.

Arados, Phoenicia, c. 400–350 B. C.

35.   Rev. Galley on waves ; above, Phoenician letters for אר='ex Arado,' to left of which, ankh, Fig. 71. 2.
Æ tetrobol.   Berlin.   Pl. XIX. 30.
B. M. C. Phoenicia, Pl. XXXVIII. 2.

36. Similar, with only first letter visible, to left of which, ankh, Fig. 71. 6.
Æ 0.78 gr.   London.   Pl. XIX. 31.
B. M. C. Phoenicia, Pl. II. 9.

Alexander the Great, 336–323 B. C.

37. Rev. Club; below, ΑΛΕΞΑΝΔΡΟY; above, ankh, Fig. 71. 2.   (Obv. Head
of Herakles in lion's skin to r.)
Æ 20mm.   Newell.

This apparently unpublished type has just come to light from a
small find of coins unearthed in Cyprus.   The provenance and symbol
mark it definitely as one of the Cypriote issues of Alexander's coinage.
Mr. Newell, who has acquired the small parcel of coins (all bronze)
from this find, and by whose kind permission the piece is here noted,
states that the style would indicate a date c. 320 B. C. for this coin.

Successors of Alexander the Great.   Uncertain Mint on the Cilician or Phoenician coast.
Philip III Arrhidaios, 323–316 B. C.

38. Rev. Zeus seated to l. on a throne, holding eagle and scepter; ΒΑΣΙΛΕΩΣ,
below; ΦΙΛΙΠΠΟY, downwards in r. field ; in l. field, ΔΑ, below which, ankh, Fig. 71.
9 ; under throne, Ι.
Æ tetradrachm.   Newell.   Pl. XX. 1.

This coin is also a probably unpublished type which Mr. Newell
assigns to an undetermined mint located somewhere along the coast of
Cilicia or Phoenicia.   The form of the ankh is unique for Greek coins.
A fairly close parallel may be found on the Syro-Hittite cylinder,
Fig. 69. 3.

Seleukos I Nikator, 316–310 B. C.

39. Rev. Similar type, but different style ; ΣΕΛΕYΚΟY downwards in r. field ;
beneath the throne, star ; in l field, Σ, above which, ankh, Fig. 71. 6.
Æ tetradrachm.   16.90 gr.   Newell.   Pl. XX. 2.
Cat. Prowe, Egger XLV, Pl. XVIII. 626.

This form of the ankh (of which that on the preceding coin may
be only a variant) is found only at Cyprus, Pl. XIX. 9, and in Phoenicia, Pl. XIX. 29, 31.   Mr. Newell informs me that he would place
this coin after c. 305 B. C.

The ankh also occurs frequently as a punchmark on coins of
Athens, on Persian sigloi, etc. which had circulated in Cilicia, as is most
interestingly shown in the case of the Cilician find noted above (Num.
Chron. 1914, p. 5, Fig. 1).   There are a great many varieties of the
sign among the punchmarks, of which nos. 4, 6, 8, 9, 19, 20, 30 and

38 (ib. Fig. 1) are certainly the ankh, while nos. 1, 16 (=27, inverted),
32 and 33 may also represent this symbol. Similar countermarks may
be seen on the edges of early electrum coins, uncertain of Southern
Ionia. A countermark on an uncertain coin of Cilicia (?), B. M. C.
Lycia, Pl. XLIV. 19, seems to be the ankh of the form, Fig. 71. 8,
found at an early date in Lycia. Also a stater of Aspendos, Fig. 74

Fig. 74.

B. M. C. Lycia, Pl. XIX. 14, shows a punchmark which may well be
the ankh (cf. Num. Chron. 1914, Fig. I. 1).

Parthia, Phraates IV, 38/37–3/2 B. C.

40. Rev. Ankh, resembling Fig. 71. 4.
Æ 8mm. London. Pl. XX. 3.
B. M. C. Parthia, Pl. XXIII. 5.

41. Rev. Ankh, Fig. 71. 8.
Æ 9mm. London. Pl. XX. 4.
Ib. Pl. XXIII. 6.

Volagases I, 51–77/78 A. D.

42. Ankh, Fig. 71. 4.
Æ 11mm. London. Pl. XX. 5.
Ib. Pl. XXIX. 13.

Volagases III, 147/8–191 A. D.

43. Similar.
Æ 19mm. London. Pl. XX. 6.
Ib. Pl. XXXV. 3.

44. Similar.
Æ 19mm. London. Pl. XX. 7.
Ib. Pl. XXXV. 5.

Persia. The Sassanidae. Varahran I, 271–274 A. D.

45. Rev. Flaming altar between two standing armed figures; on the altar,
ankh, Fig. 71. 10.
Æ drachm (or dirhem). Newell. Pl. XX. 8.

Varahran II, 274–291 A. D.

46. Similar; in upper r. field, ankh, Fig. 71. 10.
Æ drachm. Newell. Pl. XX. 9.

Narses, 291–300 A. D.

47.   Similar; in upper l. field, ankh, Fig. 71. 10; in upper r. field, symbol resembling Indian ‘taurine symbol,’ Fig. 75. 6.

Æ drachm.   Newell.   Pl. XX. 10.

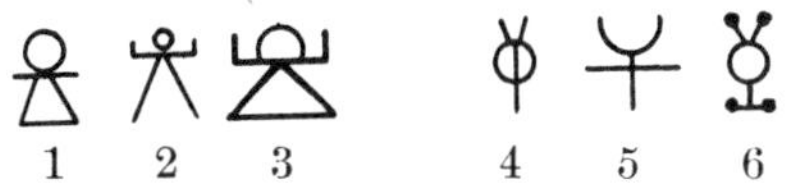

1   2   3   4   5   6

Fig. 75.

Symbols Perhaps Allied to the Ankh

Uncertain.   Olbia (?), Pamphylia.   Early Fifth Century B. C.

48.   Obv. Nude, winged male figure running to l., ankles winged; before his
face, symbol, Fig. 75. 4.   Rev. Lion to l. with head reverted; undetermined inscription; on tip of the lion's tail, same symbol as on the obverse.

Æ stater.   11.70 gr.   London.   Pl. XX. 11.

B. M. C. Lycia, Pl. XXIII. 14.

49.   Obv. Similar; symbol, Fig. 75. 4, in l. field below wing of the running
figure.   Rev. Similar.

Æ triobol.   2.91 gr.   Jameson.   Pl. XX. 12.

Coll. R. Jameson, Pl. LXXX. 1596.

The symbol on the obverse of no. 49 lacks the horizontal bar at the
base, the form given in the B. M. C. for the sign on the reverse of no. 48.
The sign as we have drawn it in Fig. 75. 4, would therefore seem to be
correct.   Also, from this same coin, no. 49, it becomes obvious that the
description of the obverse sign of no. 48 (and of that on a correspond-
ing type directed to the r., B. M. C. Lycia, Pl. XXIII. 14) as a caduceus,
is erroneous.   It is one and the same symbol on obverse and reverse,
and in the case of the type to the r. (B. M. C. Lycia, Pl. XXIII. 14)
it is probably not held by the running figure, but merely placed above
the wing as on no. 48.

Lycia, Tänägurä, c. 450–420 B. C.

50.   Obv. Winged and horned lion to l.; on his back, symbol, Fig. 75. 5.

Æ stater.   8.43 gr.   London.   Pl. XX. 13.

B. M. C. Lycia, Pl. V. 2. (cf. ib. p.xxxiii).

The reverse of this stater bears the same symbol repeated (twice
at least) in the angles of the triskeles which forms the reverse type.   A
perfect example of the sign is that on the reverse of the stater shown
in Babelon's Traité II², Pl. XCIII. 24.

India. Bactria, Indo-Parthian Line. Gondophares

51. Obv. The king on horseback to r. ; in r. field, symbol, Fig. 75. 6, the so-called ' taurine symbol.'

Billon 24mm.   Pl. XX. 14.

cf. B. M. C. Bactria, Pl. XXII. 5, 6, 8, 9, and Pl. XXII. 12, with symbol as type of reverse.

Now we have no evidence for connecting these signs with the ankh, whether as derivatives or variants. But it seems significant that we find nos. 4 and 5 of Fig. 75 associated with the figure of a lion in two cases, namely, in Pamphylia and Lycia. It would be easy to demonstrate that the lion is often a solar emblem, and to this point we shall return in a subsequent paper. What we may reasonably infer is that these signs, bearing some resemblance to the ankh, like the second symbol on the Sassanian coin, Pl. XX. 10 (upper r. field), were perhaps of the same nature as the ankh. At all events they were potent symbols, and when we come to examine their psychological content, we shall find that they belong in a class with the ankh. The ' taurine symbol ' so common on Indian coins, Fig. 75. 6, had probably the same value, and we should remember that the name given it is merely a conjecture as to the origin of the figure, and does not disclose the real nature of the sign. It is more than likely derived from the ankh or an allied symbol as found on Greek coins.

The Baal Sign

The symbol known as the Baal Sign occurs frequently on Phoenician monuments, and on coins struck by the Carthaginians in Sicily, and at Carthage, also in Numidia ; and finally it occurs on coins of the island of Cossura off Sicily, due in this latter instance also to Phoenician influence (Pl. XX. 15-19). The form which it takes is variable. Fig. 75. 1-3 gives the chief varieties found on coins. The figure found on the monuments resembles most frequently that found on the coin of Cossura, Pl. XX. 19, Fig. 75. 3. Illustrations are given in Goblet d'Alviella's work, Figs. 40 and 103, from stelai found in Libya. On a silver diadem from Batna in Algeria (Cook, Zeus, Pl. XXVI. 3) bearing the busts of Tanit, the north-African form of the great Phoenician mother-goddess, Astarte, and of Ba' al-Hamman, widely worshiped in the same region, a crudely drawn symbol (to r. of caduceus)[1] may also be a variant of the Baal sign. This seems to be an anthropomorphized Baal sign. Many of the stelai of Carthage bearing the sign are dedi-

---

[1] Goblet d'Alviella, *op. cit.*, Fig. 106.

cated to Tanit so that we may infer that the symbol belonged to the goddess as well as to her consort, Ba' al-Hamman. The bibliography of the subject will be found in the works here cited.

The Baal Sign on Greek Coins
Liculo-Punic.   Uncertain Mint, c. 410–310 B. C.

1. Rev. Quadriga; in front of the charioteer, Baal sign, Fig. 75. 1.
Æ tetradrachm.   16.51 gr.   Jameson.   Pl. XX. 15.
Coll. R. Jameson, Pl. XXXV. 730.

2. Obv. Head of Persephone to r.; in l. field, Baal sign, Fig. 75. 2.
Æ tetradrachm.   16.71 gr. (formerly Benson).   Pl. XX. 16.
Cat. Benson, Pl. XXVI. 799.   cf. L. Müller, Numismatique de l'Ancienne Afrique, p. 77, no. 32, with form of sign, Fig. 75. 1 (Berlin).

3. Rev. Free horse prancing to r.; above, Baal sign, Fig. 75. 1.
N 7.64 gr.   London.   Pl. XX. 17.
Hill, Sicily, Pl. X. 9.   Head, H. N². p. 877.

Thabraca and Tuniza, Numidia, Second to First Century, B. C.
4. Rev. Beardless head with ringlets; in r. field, Baal sign, Fig. 75. 1.
Æ 24mm.   London.   Pl. XX. 18.
Head, H. N². p. 886.

Cossura, Island off Sicily, Second Half of First Century B. C.
5. Rev. COSSVRA within a wreath of laurel; above, Baal sign, Fig. 75. 3.
Æ 27mm.   London.   Pl. XX. 19.
Hill, Sicily, Pl. XV. 18.

From the form of the sign found on coins of Askalon in Palestine, associated with the figure of Phanebal, one is tempted to infer that this is another instance of the Baal sign.   The coin, Fig. 76, is a late im-

Fig. 76.

perial bronze (B. M. C. Palestine, Pl. XIII. 18), but scarcely well enough preserved to determine the precise form of the sign in the l. field.

The symbol on the coins of Melita (Malta) bearing the head of Isis, Fig. 77, is described as a caduceus and ankh combined (Head, H. N². p. 883).   But this description seems inaccurate, the symbol suggesting rather the Baal sign and caduceus combined, though this is not an entirely probable interpretation either.

The Baal sign was very probably derived from the ankh. The latter of course was thoroughly familiar to the Phoenicians whose art shows many borrowings from Egyptian symbolism; the winged disk,

Fig. 77.

as we shall see, being a case in point. The swastika also we have seen appropriated by them from earlier art. Furthermore, the ankh on a bronze coin of Euagoras II, 361-351 B. C., King of Salamis, Cyprus, Fig. 78 (B. M. C. Cyprus, Pl. XII. 6), actually takes the form of the Baal

Fig. 78.

sign, Fig. 75. 1. The form of the ankh on this piece is exceptional in the Cypriote series, but there can be no doubt that it is simply a variant of this sign.

THE WINGED DISK

The winged disk is, like the ankh, original with the Egyptians. It occurs as early as the Sixth Dynasty (Cook, Zeus, p. 205, note 1, where bibliography is given) on a triumphal stele of Pepi I.[1] It is seen in highly artistic form on monuments of the Eighteenth Dynasty (cf. Cook, ib. Fig. 149). The device was commonly placed on the pylons (cf. the pylon-shaped pectoral, Pl. XVIII. 3, where a portion is visible), or gateways, of temple-courts. The Phoenicians copied this custom of placing the winged disk on the lintels of temples. The object of the custom was to consecrate the buildings by placing the sacred sign upon them as a protective emblem, as is expressly stated in the Egyptian Myth of the Winged Disk (Cook, ib. p. 206). The name borne by this emblem and its exact meaning is not settled, but the popular term ‘ mihr,’ the Persian appellation, is commonly used.

The form of the emblem undergoes many changes as it passes from Egyptian into Assyrian, Phoenician and Persian art. Fig. 79. *a-i*, from

---

[1] Ward, Seal Cylinders, p. 395, quoting Sayce, says the Fifth Dynasty.

Ward (*op. cit.*, p. 396) illustrates a number of these variations drawn chiefly from cylinders, except *h* which is taken from the figure given in Lepsius, Denkmäler III, Pl. 3b. Of these varieties, *a*, *b*, *d*, *e*, *g*, and *i* are Assyrian, while *c* and *f* are Persian. Ward states that the symbol is probably not found in Assyrian art until after the invasion of the

Fig. 79. *a–i*.

Eighteenth Dynasty, but may be earlier in Syria and Phoenicia. The Phoenician form of the winged disk is particularly interesting when compared with the figure which the device takes on the coins of Carthage. Fig. 80. 1, 2 (Goblet d'Alviella, Fig. 113, from Renan, Mission de Phénicie, Pl. LV, and Fig. 134) shows the disk almost divested of the extensive wings of the original Egyptian emblem, Fig. 79. *h*, and showing prominently the two uraeus-snakes. On the Greek coins of Cyprus and Cilicia (Pl. XX. 20-22), on the other hand, the uraeus-

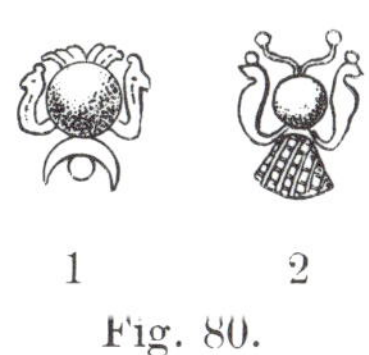

1   2

Fig. 80.

snakes have virtually disappeared, totally, we may say, unless the curvilinear appendages are the last vestiges of the serpents, as is probably the case.

The Egyptian figure, Fig. 79. *h*, is composed of a disk flanked by two uraeus-snakes enclosed within broad wings extending laterally. The wings are usually called those of a sparrow-hawk, but Cook prefers to call them those of a falcon (*op. cit.*, p. 205, note 1). From Fig. 149 given by Cook, it is plain that the undulating lines across the wings are meant to represent the serpents' tails, and not, as Goblet d'Alviella wrote, the horns of a goat. This fact is also very clearly indicated in the Assyrian winged disk shown in Fig. 81 (Ward, *op. cit.*, p. 217, Fig.

Fig. 81.

655) from a cylinder on which a female figure is represented in a typical attitude beneath the disk. Here there is but one serpent which lies partly coiled, extended above the disk and wings.

The elements of the figure are therefore simply, disk, serpents and wings. This composite figure blends three solar pictures in one, the direct picture of the sun's orb and two solar analogues, the bird and serpent. On the full significance of these solar devices in their psychological import we shall dwell later.

Fig. 82.

The winged disk of the Egyptians gave rise to the winged disk or 'sign' of Ashur, patron deity of the city of Ashur and chief god of the Assyrians. This emblem shows the half-figure of the god, ' the tail serves him for a kilt ' (Cook), enclosed within the winged disk, as seen in Fig. 82, an Assyrian cylinder representing the king and winged attendant approaching the sacred tree, or tree of life, surmounted by the disk of Ashur. From Assyrian art the sign of Ashur passed over into Persia where it was adopted as the emblem of Ahuramazda (Cook, *op. cit.*, Fig. 153). This is the figure which appears as reverse type on certain coins of Cilicia, Pl. XX. 23, and on the coins of Persis, where it is placed above the sacred fire-altar, Pl. XX. 28.

The Winged Disk on Greek Coins
Paphos, Cyprus. Stasandros, c. 450 B. C.

1. Obv. Bull standing to l.; above, winged disk composed of globe, drooping wings and tail feathers; in front, ankh.
    Æ stater. 10.91 gr. London. Pl. XX. 20.
    B. M. C. Cyprus, Pl. VII. 13.

Tarsos, Cilicia. Satrap Datames, 378–372 B. C.

2. Rev. Satrap in Persian dress seated to r. on throne, examining an arrow; in field above, winged disk with tail feathers and curved appendages, lower part duplicated above the globe.
    Æ stater. 10.30 gr. London. Pl. XX. 21.
    B. M. C. Cilicia, Pl. XXIX. 11.

Mallos, Cilicia, c. 385–333 B. C.

3. Rev. Male figure in long chiton driving a yoke of oxen to l.; in field above, winged disk of form similar to that of no. 1.
    Æ stater. 10.10 gr. London. Pl. XX. 22.
    B. M. C. Cilicia, Pl. XVII. 1.

Issos, Cilicia. Satrap Tiribazos, c. 386–380 B. C.

4. Rev. Ahuramazda, to front, nude, head to r., his body terminates in a winged disk of Persian form, central disk, wings, tail feathers and scrolls.
    Æ stater. 10.29 gr. London. Pl. XX. 23.
    B. M. C. Cilicia, Pl. XV. 3.

With this coin compare the issue of Tiribazos at Tarsos, Fig. 83

Fig. 83.

(B. M. C. Cilicia, Pl. XXIX. 1) which shows the polos on the god's head.

Satrapal (?) Coin of Phoenicia (?), c. 390 B. C.

5. Rev. Ahuramazda to r., wearing turreted crown, body terminates in a solar disk with four wings.

Æ stater.   12.12 gr.   Newell.   Pl. XX. 24.

Newell, Num. Chron. 1914, Pl. IV. 5.

This unique coin is regarded by its owner as a satrapal issue struck in some city along the Phoenician coast. The style of the winged figure suggests the Persian satrapal coinage of Tiribazos, and the representation is doubtless Ahuramazda as on the preceding coins.

Carthage, Zeugitana, c. 241–146 B. C.

6. Rev. Horse standing to r. ; above, winged disk of Phoenician form with two uraeus-snakes crowned with solar disks, the globe seemingly surrounded by rays.

El. 11.33 gr.   Newell.   Pl. XX. 25.

7. Rev. Similar.

Æ 25mm.   Newell.   Pl. XX. 26.

8. Rev. Similar ; the serpents have practically vanished.

Æ 18mm.   Newell.   Pl. XX. 27.

On no. 8 the winged disk has degenerated into what is practically a radiate disk bearing no resemblance in itself to its distant prototype in Egyptian art. The two preceding types, however, nos. 6 and 7, foreshadowed this metamorphosis. We may then perhaps be justified in tracing the ' star ' symbol above the identical type on a later coin, Fig. 84, a silver tetradrachm of Carthage to the winged disk, and in

Fig. 84.

calling this ' star ' sign a ' sun.' This is often the meaning of this symbol as has been shown by P. Gardner in his paper, Ares as a Sun-God, Num. Chron. 1880. We have noted above the resemblance between the winged disk on Carthaginian coins and Phoenician monuments.

Persis.   Autophradates I

9. Rev. Persian fire-altar, surmounted by an image of Ahuramazda.

Æ tetradrachm.   16.95 gr.   Pl. XX. 28.

Allotte de la Füye, La Numismatique de la Perside (Corolla Numismatica), Pl. III. 18.

In conclusion of this section we may note the following instances of the Egyptian solar disk, not the winged disk, but a variant of the Egyptian sun-symbol which has an interest for our general argument since it shows that the serpents were an important element in the concept. Fig. 85, a coin of Alexandria in Egypt, shows the goddess Isis holding the infant Horos, within a temple, while in the pediment is a disk with uraeus-serpents, in a composition which recalls the head-

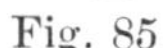

Fig. 85.   Fig. 86.

dress of Isis, another solar emblem, the sun's disk between two bull's horns. The device on this coin seems, however, to be a globe and serpents. Fig. 86, a coin of Aspendos (B. M. C. Pl. XXII. 11), shows a shrine enclosing two cultus-statues, in the pediment of which is a globe between two serpents confronting. Like the winged disk, this serpent-flanked disk was placed in the pediment as an apotropaion, or protective emblem. For a parallel representation on Greek vases, and its gradual degeneration into a mere central disk or shield, see Cook, Zeus, pp. 293ff. On Greek imperial coins the globe often seen in the pediments of temples may be a survival from the Egyptian disk.

THE SWASTIKA, TRISKELES, ETC., ANKH AND WINGED DISK AS LIBIDO SYMBOLS

We come now to the psychological aspect of symbolism, having passed in review the archaeological material. In our introduction we discussed a symbol of great interest to modern people because of its use by the early Christians and its hitherto enigmatical character. It was there shown that no satisfactory solution of the equation Christ=Fish had previously been proposed, although the fact of the symbolic use of the Fish in the eucharist had been demonstrated. Our argument, however, led to the conclusion that the identification of Christ with the Fish preceded the eucharistic symbolism. The underlying meaning of the analogy Christ=Fish was found revealed in the heathen-Christian legend of the birth of Christ from the Spring, or Fountain, an analogue for the 'Mother,' — a legend which is a mere variant of the numerous symbolic tales of Immaculate Conception. Jung says (*op. cit.*, p. 190) '' The fish is the symbol of the child, for the child lives before its birth in water like the fish.'' The Libido nature of this symbolism is therefore apparent.

It shall be our next effort to demonstrate that the symbols above described, the swastika, triskeles, etc., the ankh and the winged disk, became potent and magic signs because they too are expressions of the vital thing in human life, which is the human Libido. The significance of the word Libido, and the meaning of the Libido symbolism are difficult to define adequately as well as somewhat subtle to comprehend, and we shall not attempt now to formulate any further definitions, but refer the reader once more to the sources noted in our introduction. Yet without defining the Libido symbol we can talk about it and thus gain a knowledge of its meaning.

The swastika, as we have seen, is somewhat obscure to us as regards original meaning. Nevertheless it came to be, if indeed it was not always, a symbol for the sun like the analogous figures, the triskeles and Lycian symbol. It is less probably to be derived from the solar wheel, and is more reasonably interpreted as an expression for the sun in motion, sun's limbs, like the other 'turning' symbols. All these figures taken by themselves might be held in theory to represent the abstract concept 'speed,' but their use on the monuments leads to the conclusion that they are pictorial images of a concrete thing in nature, the ever-moving sun.

Now solar symbolism is a well-known phenomenon to the student of ancient art and religion. To the modern mind, not conversant with the theory of symbolism set forth by the psychoanalytic school of psychologists, the only explanation for solar worship, solar religion, would be the vivid impression made by the sun, the most conspicuous of the heavenly bodies, upon primitive man. This is true as far as it goes, but it is not the whole of the matter. Other natural phenomena besides the sun and its movement have made an equally vivid impression upon primitive man, in fact upon all mankind at certain stages of their development, and constitute a universal and fecund source for poetic, artistic and religious symbolism. But the mainspring of all the different forms of symbolism created by the unconscious is the inner psychic nature of man which is determined and governed by the Libido. To the normal mind in its conscious activity, a tree is a tree, but to earlier mankind the tree was a powerful symbol. It stood for Life, and the intricacies and far-reaching nature of the tree symbolism in art and religion at different epochs is a marvellous chapter in human psychology. Jung has shown that the tree is likewise a symbol for the 'Mother,' and that it may have a phallic significance.

Furthermore, it is not merely primitive man who creates such symbolisms. Psychoanalysis has proved that such symbolism is present in the unconscious life of modern man. To understand all this thoroughly, it is necessary to comprehend the Psychology of the Unconscious as evolved by Jung and his school. In the realm of unconscious phantasy there is no such thing as a fixed concrete meaning. Jung (*op. cit.*, p. 215) says " The only reality there, is the Libido; to it every phenomenon is only an analogue." The sun's daily course in the heavens is conceived as a birth and rebirth. The sun sails above the sea into which it dips every evening (sea=the Mother), and every day it once more arises and is born again. Upon this symbolic conception of birth and rebirth, all the solar myths hinge. The sun is the Undying God to which the heroes are likened. The Libido symbolism of the sun has wide application in the myths and art of all peoples. Solar symbolism however is only one manifestation of the more extensive Libido symbolism. The phenomenon of symbolism is described by Jung as an act of transference of the Libido on the road to sublimation. The fixation of the Libido, and the necessity for transference are the primary causes for symbolism.

The ankh is a symbol of less wide-spread usage than the swastika, but its antiquity is apparently as great. Like other Egyptian hieroglyphs it probably had its pictographic predecessor, but as a matter of fact we know no earlier form of the sign than that shown in Fig. 71. 1. We have traced its survival down to the Fifth Century A. D., and it may quite possibly occur on Egyptian monuments of more recent date. Like the swastika it has not entirely disappeared even in modern times, and still retains traces of its original significance. For example, it is used as an astronomical symbol, standing for the planet Venus, and in biological works it is employed as a symbol signifying 'female.'

The ankh is a Libido symbol *par excellence*, for, as has been stated, its meaning as a hieroglyph is ' life,' ' to live.' This concept by a natural extension came to include the idea of immortality, as is evidenced on many monuments where the symbol is held out towards a mummy in token of resurrection.   Hence it is the symbol of paramount significance in Egyptian art and religion, the favorite emblem of gods and kings.   Symbols and phantasies of life and immortality are bound up in the Libido, as Jung has amply demonstrated.   The manifestations of this symbolism are infinitely varied.   Light, fire, flame, the sun, sun's rays, etc., are in turn equated with life, and enter into poetic and artistic phantasy as expressions of the Libido.

The winged disk is also a Libido symbol for it is an image of the sun, the source of life and life-giving energy.   As a sun symbol we have traced it from Egyptian through Assyrian into Persian and Phoenician art.   In Assyrian and Persian art we found it incorporated into the representations of the national sun-gods, Ashur and Ahuramazda. As compared with the swastika and the ankh, its usage is far more restricted both chronologically and geographically.

In conclusion it is interesting to observe that the most potent of the symbols here discussed, namely, the Christian Ichthys-symbol, the swastika, ankh and winged disk were used as prophylakteria or protective emblems — a usage which has been called the common fate of all symbols.   This usage, however, should not be considered as the ' latter-day fate ' of the symbol, viewed historically, but should rather be understood as inherent in the nature of a powerful symbol.   Zmigrodski declared that he had seen the swastika in modern Italy over the huts of fishermen, but we have shown that the talismanic or protective use of the swastika was also known in ancient Greek art (cf. Figs. 31. 32).   Egyptian amulets or charms often take the form of the ankh, and the winged disk was from the first placed as a protective emblem over the entrances to temples.

From our analysis of these symbols as Libido analogues, it follows that there is no ground for the opinion widely entertained by writers on symbolism that all of these symbols were originally, or even commonly, conceived as phallic.   We hold that a symbol should only be designated as phallic when it is clear that it actually has this more limited application, e. g., the ankh on the relief of the temple of Luxor. But we need not score too heavily the earlier interpreters as having wholly erred, for they often use the word ' phallic ' apparently for want of a better term.   In fact, they seem to have realized instinctively from the study of symbols in general, their Libido character.

AGNES BALDWIN.

107

18

19

20

THE SWASTIKA ON GREEK VASES

THE SWASTIKA, GREEK COINS, 1-26; INDIAN COINS, 27-37

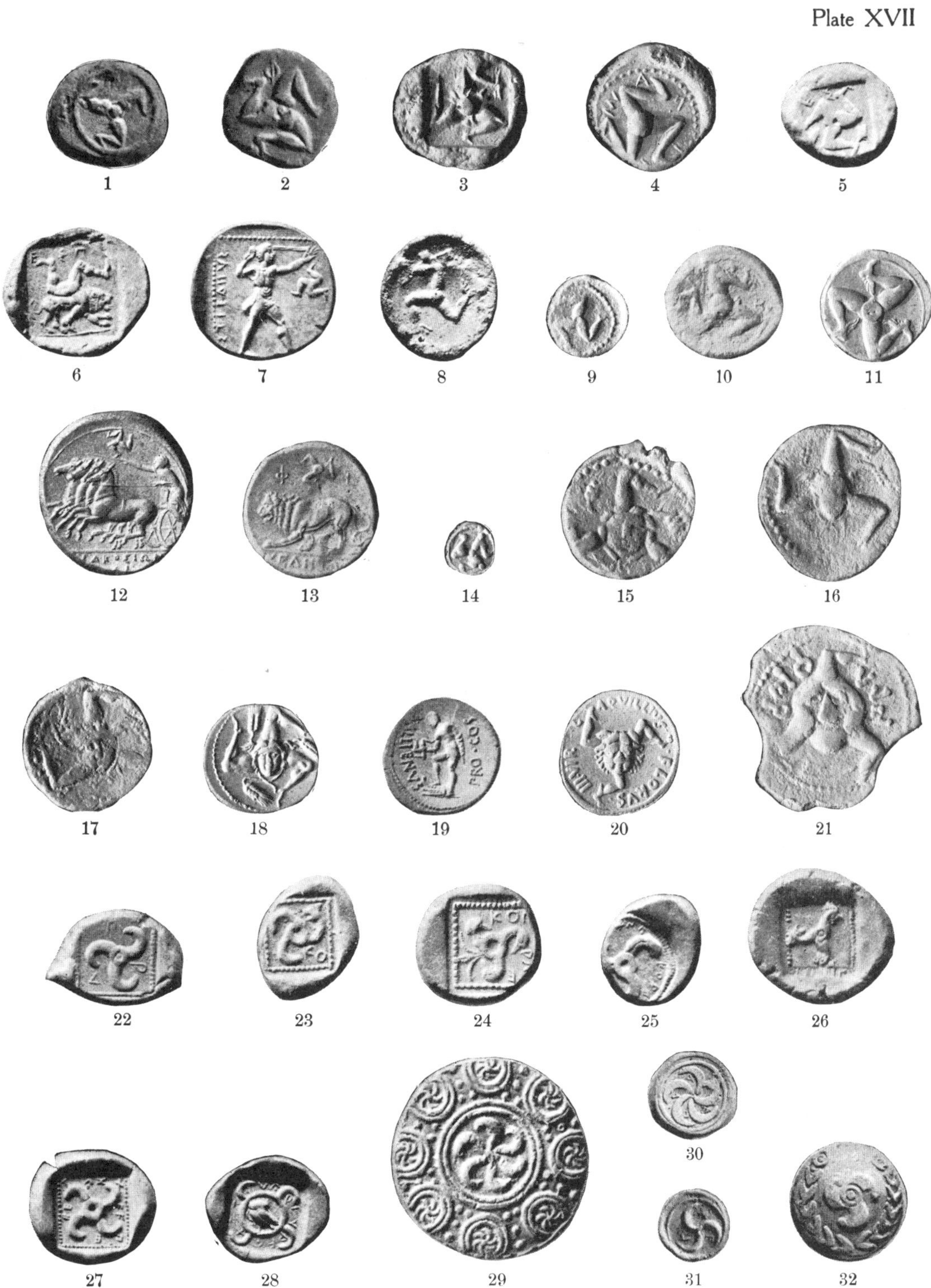

THE TRISKELES, 1-21; LYCIAN SYMBOL, 22-32 — GREEK COINS

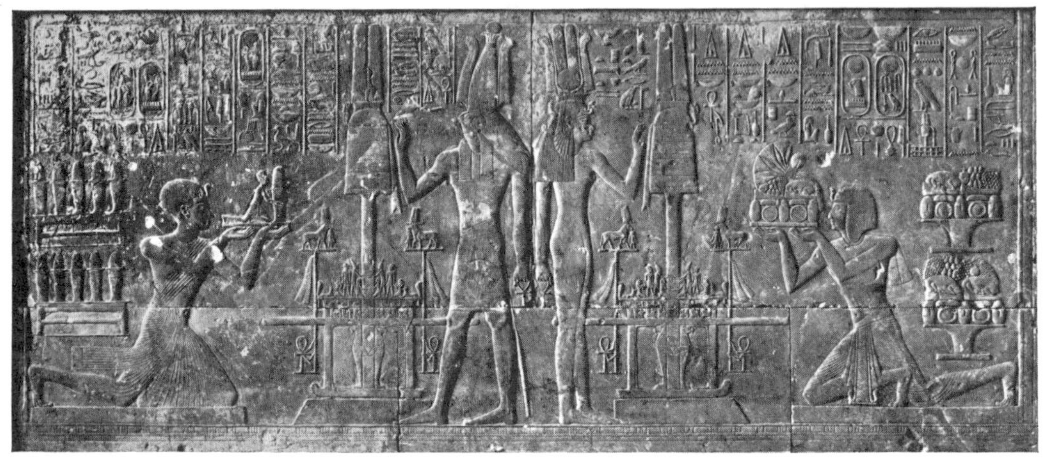

1

2

3

THE ANKH ON EGYPTIAN MONUMENTS

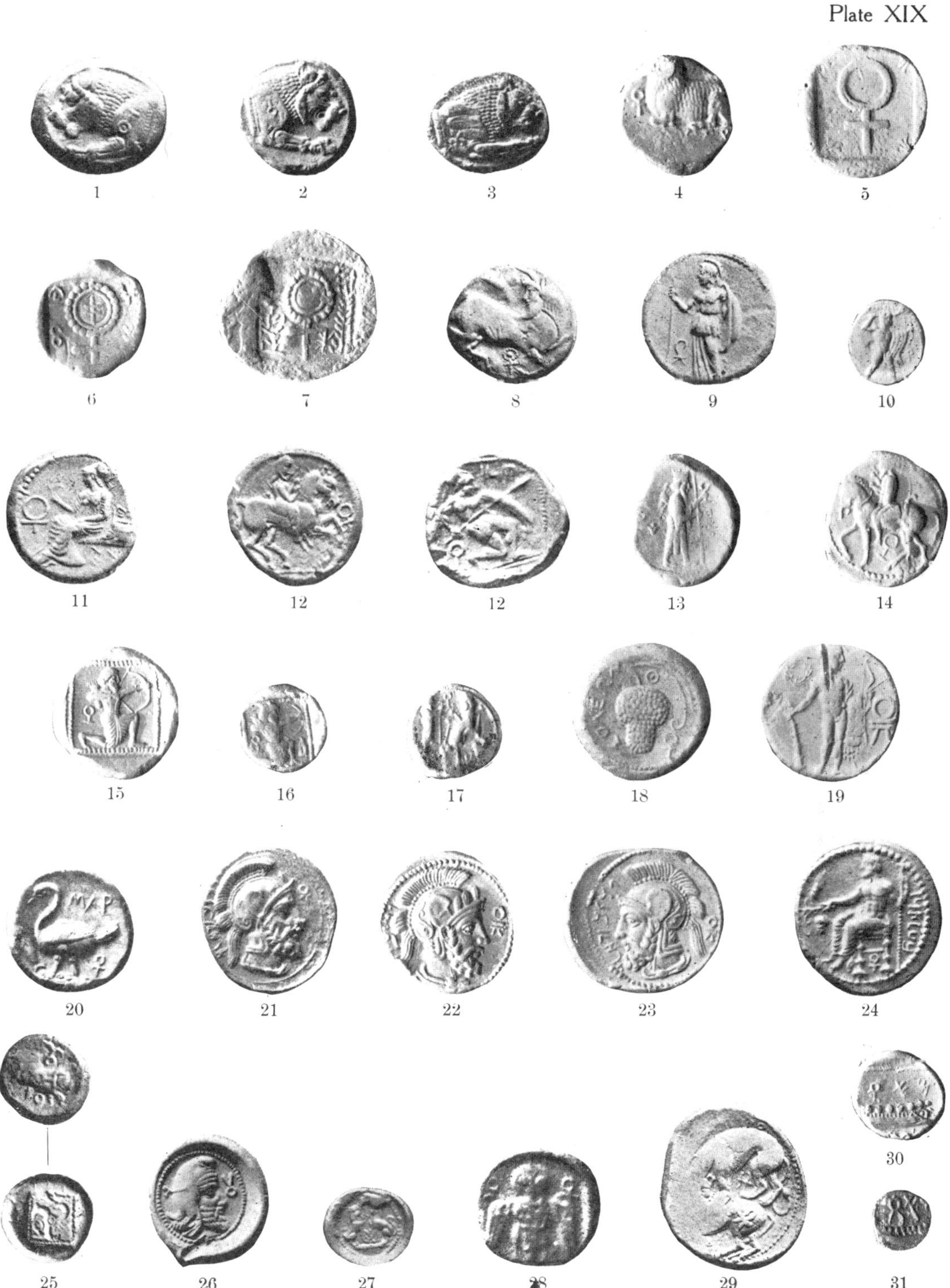

THE ANKH, 1-31,— GREEK COINS

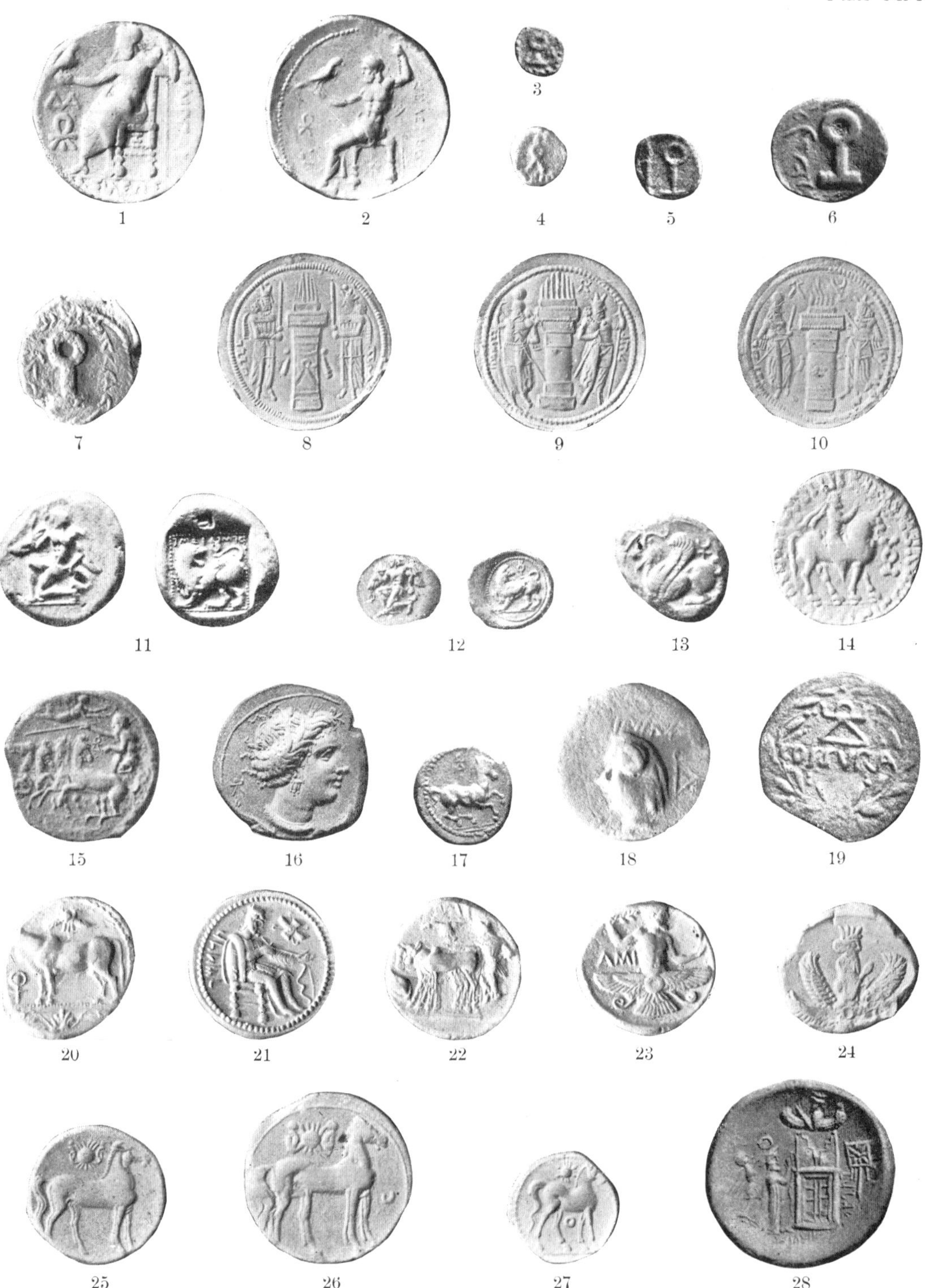

THE ANKH, 1-10, AND ALLIED SIGNS, 11-14; THE BAAL SIGN, 15-19;
THE WINGED DISK, 20-28, — GREEK COINS